Korean War
A Captivating Guide to Korean War History

© **Copyright 2017**

All rights Reserved. No part of this book may be reproduced in any form without permission in writing from the author. Reviewers may quote brief passages in reviews.

Disclaimer: No part of this publication may be reproduced or transmitted in any form or by any means, mechanical or electronic, including photocopying or recording, or by any information storage and retrieval system, or transmitted by email without permission in writing from the publisher.

While all attempts have been made to verify the information provided in this publication, neither the author nor the publisher assumes any responsibility for errors, omissions or contrary interpretations of the subject matter herein.

This book is for entertainment purposes only. The views expressed are those of the author alone, and should not be taken as expert instruction or commands. The reader is responsible for his or her own actions.

Adherence to all applicable laws and regulations, including international, federal, state and local laws governing professional licensing, business practices, advertising and all other aspects of doing business in the US, Canada, UK or any other jurisdiction is the sole responsibility of the purchaser or reader.

Neither the author nor the publisher assumes any responsibility or liability whatsoever on the behalf of the purchaser or reader of these materials. Any perceived slight of any individual or organization is purely unintentional.

Contents

FREE BONUS FROM CAPTIVATING HISTORY (AVAILABLE FOR A LIMITED TIME) 5

INTRODUCTION 6

CHAPTER 1 – THE JAPANESE ASCENDENCY: 1910-1945 8

CHAPTER 2 – A KOREA DIVIDED: THE US OCCUPATION OF THE SOUTH 21

CHAPTER 3 – THE FORGING OF THE NORTH KOREAN STATE 37

CHAPTER 4 –FIRST BLOOD: THE OUTBREAK OF WAR 44

CHAPTER 5 – STRIKE HARD AND STRIKE FAST: THE US RETREAT 59

CHAPTER 6 – BITTERSWEET VICTORIES: AMERICAN REVIVAL AND CHINA'S DECISION TO CROSS THE YALU 69

CHAPTER 7 – HOW DO YOU SOLVE A PROBLEM LIKE CHINA? 83

CHAPTER 8 – THE BLOODY CEASEFIRE AND LOOMING BOMB **91**

CHAPTER 9 – THE LEGACY OF THE KOREAN WAR **100**

CONCLUSION **109**

PREVIEW OF WORLD WAR 2 114

A CAPTIVATING GUIDE FROM BEGINNING TO END 114

FREE BONUS FROM CAPTIVATING HISTORY (AVAILABLE FOR A LIMITED TIME) **124**

SOURCES **125**

Free Bonus from Captivating History (Available for a Limited time)

Hi History Lovers!

Now you have a chance to join our exclusive history list so you can get your first history ebook for free as well as discounts and a potential to get more history books for free! Simply visit the link below to join.

Captivatinghistory.com/ebook

Also, make sure to follow us on:

Twitter: @Captivhistory

Facebook: Captivating History: @captivatinghistory

Introduction

The narrative of the Korean War in the West, and particularly in the United States, tells the tale of a conflict between two global superpowers and competing ideologies in a far-flung corner of the globe.

The reality is that the wheels of motion that drove the country to war in 1950 began turning long before American boots set foot on Korean soil. The heart of the conflict was a civil war between a population arbitrarily divided by colonization and the global geopolitics at the end of the Second World War.

Challenging the widely perpetuated Western narrative and getting to the core of the Korean conflict is no easy feat. From assumptions that the outbreak of war was a deliberate act of communist aggression, to the notion that Eisenhower and Truman's constant threats of atomic annihilation broke the Chinese and North Korean spirit and led to the signing of the armistice, everything needs to be dissected and reviewed on its own factual merit to fully understand the nature of the war.

This guide seeks to pull this narrative curtain and peek behind at the truth of the matter, tracing the history of the war back to the Japanese occupation and uncovering the root of Korean nationalism that stirred the nation into the frenzy of civil war in 1950.

It is about an often-forgotten war, fighting for its place in history between the two behemoths of the Second World War and the Vietnam War, which was no less significant, no less destructive, and had no less impact on the global politics of the twentieth century.

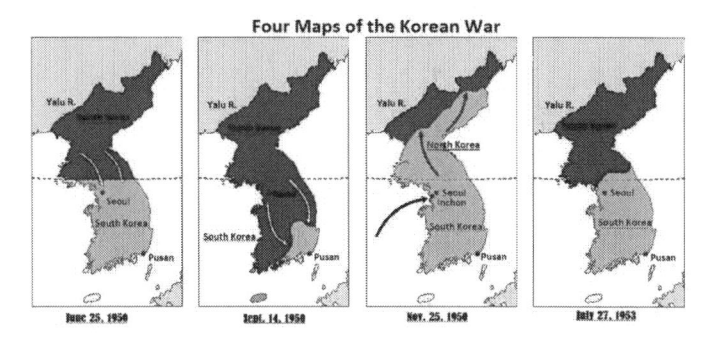

Four Maps of the Korean War

Chapter 1 – The Japanese Ascendency: 1910–1945

The chain of events that brought the Korean peninsula to the outbreak of war in 1950 can be traced back to almost half a century before, at the beginning of the Japanese occupation of the country. The Korean nation, with a shared culture, language, ethnicity and heritage, deteriorated from harmonious social cohesion to a bloody civil war in just 40 years. The scars of the conflict are still etched on the Korean political landscape today. The North has a reclusive communist government, while the South has flourished as a democratic republic.

To understand the rapid deterioration and ultimate segregation of the peninsula, we must examine the conditions of the Japanese occupation of the country. Koreans under Japanese rule were a systematically divided and oppressed population. They saw their culture suppressed and their workforce mobilized to feed Japanese mouths and drive the Japanese war machine. But the period also gave birth to the Korean independence movement and began to shape Korean nationalism. Nationalist ideas would begin to be formed, both within Korea itself, across the Yalu River in China, and within the Soviet Union by those in exile. These same ideas which were bred under Japanese rule are those that gave the peninsula the political divide we can still see today.

The Japan-Korea Annexation Treaty of 1910

After formally becoming a Japanese protectorate in 1905 and handing over control of administrative affairs to the Japanese in 1907, Japanese Resident General Count Terauchi Masatake drew up the Japan-Korea Annexation Treaty in 1910, to formally transfer the governance of Korea to the Emperor of Japan. When presented with the treaty, Emperor Sunjong of Korea had no intention of signing it. But, with the ominous threat of Japanese invasion looming if he didn't, he reluctantly placed his national seal of the Korean Empire on the treaty and, rather than sign it himself, presented Prime Minister Lee Wan-yong with the document to sign[i].

Sunjong faced the dilemma of either signing the document and accepting Japanese rule, or resist and be taken by force, which would undoubtedly have left many casualties and led to a more submissive relationship under the Japanese government. The fact the Emperor himself didn't actually sign the document, and the conditions of duress that the document was presented under, has led many subsequent governments of both South and North Korea to question the legality of the treaty.

Life under Japanese rule

Despite the Emperor's seal, the Koreans were treated as conquered people. The Japanese implemented their version of military rule, known as *budan seiji*[ii]. The military and police extended their control into every aspect of Korean life. Koreans were not allowed to publish their own newspapers or organize their own political groups[iii], nor were they included in high levels of government administration. Korean land was frequently confiscated by the Japanese and redistributed.

Economically, the Japanese implemented a system of protectionist capitalism. They used Korean labor to drive Japanese industries. Koreans found themselves working in Japanese-owned firms. Any profits were sent back to Japan[iv] and only a very small and select group of Korean elites became successful under Japanese rule. In 1942, Korean entrepreneurs owned just 1.5% of the total capital invested in Korean industries and they were charged interest rates up to 25% higher than their Japanese counterparts[v]. These conditions made it impossible for the Korean working class to improve their lot and eroded the wealth of the already established middle class.

The Japanese occupiers wanted to ensure total stability and control on the peninsula, which would provide a buffer area between them and Chinese aggression[vi]. Their intention was to use the Korean peninsula to expand into northeast China and take the Chinese region of Manchuria.

They used Korea to fill a grain shortage in Japan. Rice and soybeans were exported from Korea to Osaka, Yokohama, and Yagasaki[vii]. As more and more grain left the country to feed the Japanese occupiers, there was less to go around for the Korean population. Between 1932 and 1936, the rice consumption per capita in Korea was half of what it had been from 1912 to 1916[viii].

The March First Movement

But the Koreans, who had been used to self-rule within the Chinese Orbit and were proud of their cultural traditions, were a cohesive social society. A resistance movement had been forming throughout the first decade of Japanese rule and on 1 March, 1919, 33 activists publicly read a Korean Declaration of Independence in Seoul and aired their complaints on the radio and in the newspapers.

Public protests spread across the country that day and Japanese forces responded with bloodshed and violence. Korean sources claim 7,509 people were killed by Japanese military forces, while Japanese officials are adamant the figure is lower, at 553 people. The protests were suppressed through the military, but the Korean population had made a prominent statement.

The second phase of the Japanese Occupation

In the wake of the demonstrations, the Japanese occupation under Admiral Saito Makoto entered a new phase. Unlike the iron-fisted military rule of his predecessor, Makoto ushered in a period of cultural rule (*bunka seiji*)[ix]. The strict controls on Korean culture were eased, Koreans could publish their own newspapers and laws against public expression and gathering were lifted.

But the changes were short lived. In the 1930s, the military took control of the Japanese government and the Korean colony was required to play a more important role in forging a Japanese Empire. The Japanese launched their campaign into China in 1931, taking Manchuria and creating the Japanese state of Manchukuo. It was at this point the Japanese adopted a policy of assimilation towards the Korean population. Worship at Shinto Shrines became mandatory[x] and Korean families were forced to take Japanese family names. Korean schools were forbidden from using the Korean language and all education was given in Japanese.

In 1937, Japan embarked on the second Sino-Japanese War against China. The whole of the Japanese Empire was placed on war footing, including the Korean population. The Korean economy was modified to support the war effort. Heavy industries were introduced, with the construction of large scale chemical and electrical plants[xi]. The transportation systems were modified to cater for the distribution of resources and troops to Manchukuo, to the north of the peninsula. Although the profits were still being funneled back to Japan, the Sino-Japanese war was a period of intense economic development. They created Korean industries and brought the country away from merely agricultural development, which brought many benefits to the country in the years following the occupation.

The Japanese continued their efforts to strip the Korean population of any semblance of a national identity and culture and impose their own on the peninsula. By 1940, 84% of all

Korean families had adopted Japanese names, only the Japanese language was spoken in schools and in public spheres, and they had shut down all Korean newspapers and media publications after the outbreak of war[xii]. But, in doing so, the Japanese had instigated a prominent Korean nationalist movement.

The Birth of Korean Nationalism

The Japanese occupation of the Korean peninsula created the perfect conditions for a resistance movement to grow. The *yangban* (landowning class) and the urban middle class, resented the Japanese occupation and the lack of opportunities it offered. While a select few Korean elites were becoming wealthy through collaboration with the Japanese occupiers, the majority were made landless and reduced to a state of poverty by Japanese rule[xiii].

During the first phase of the occupation, the nationalist movement was focused on middle-class *yangban* students. They regularly organized protests and engaged in pro-independence activities. The movement received financial backing from some political elites of the country, like Kim Song-su, a wealthy Korean entrepreneur who made his fortunes in the textile industry. But these entrepreneurs had to be careful. They were in business with the Japanese regime and any support for independence movements was risky and needed to be discrete[xiv].

In the early occupation period, nationalist movements among the poorer rural classes manifested themselves as small flare-ups of insurrections. Calling themselves the Righteous Army, their rebellions were disorganized and were easily put down by the Japanese military throughout the 1910s and 1920s. For the rural classes, these small revolts were driven more by anger over poverty and inequality than actual nationalist ideology.

Many Korean intellectuals and nationalists were living in exile in Soviet Russia and China, after fleeing Korea during its annexation. After the October Revolution in 1917 and the perpetuation of communist ideas across Asia, the appetite to form a pro-independence, communist movement in Korea grew. In 1918, in Irkutsk, Soviet Russia, the First Korean Communist Party was formed by Koreans living in exile[xv]. Although considered part of the Russian Communist Party, it was organized as the Korean Section.

In Shanghai, the center of the Chinese working class movement, Koreans living in exile formed a Provisional Government of Korea. They also embraced socialism as a solution to Korea's problems. The Provincial

Government declared a ruling coalition with the newly formed *Koryo Communist Party[xvi]*, led by Yi Tong-hwi, a former Korean army officer. Yi Tong-hwi and his counterparts in Russia used their ties and connections to spread their socialist agenda within the Korean peninsula.

Their effort was rewarded in 1925 when the Korean Communist Party was formed, on Korean soil[xvii]. However, maintaining a national communist party in Korea was a risky business. Their charismatic leader, Pak Hon-yong, had been in the Shanghai faction in 1921 and returned to Korea to form the Korean Communist Party, aged just 25. He was imprisoned first by the Japanese Military in 1925, shortly after the formation of the party, and spent four years in prison. In 1933, he was arrested again. This time, the Japanese systematically tortured him and kept him in isolation for the next six years, to the point that they believed him to be insane and incapable of leading a movement when they released him in 1939. But he came out and reformed the party, eventually fleeing to South Cholla to avoid re-arrest[xviii].

The Provisional Government in Shanghai were also busy making preparations to re-enter Korea. Kim Ku, a prominent figure in the Provisional Government, organized high-profile assassinations of Japanese high officials. He also met with Chinese leader Chiang Kai-shek in 1933 to secure financial aid for the nationalist cause. Ku promised that in return for financial support from the Chinese Government, the Provisional Government in exile would generate uprisings against the Japanese in Japan, Korea, and Manchuria (Manchukuo) within the next two years[xix]. While Chiang Kai-shek refused to give the desired financial support, he did begin a scheme whereby the Chinese forces would train military cadets for the Korean Provisional Government[xx]. However, the scheme was abandoned a year later, after heavy protest from Japan.

In the later part of the occupation, when the Japanese embarked on their aggressive assimilation policy, the Korean nationalist movement was forced into exile once again. It became too dangerous to remain in Korea and continue operations and surviving leaders of the movements described a time of constant police surveillance and job discrimination wherever they turned[xxi]. Many went across the border into China and joined the Provisional Government in Shanghai. Some fled across the Yalu River into Japan's newly created state of Manchukuo and embarked on guerrilla operations to undermine the Japanese occupation there. Their goal was to form a people's army in Manchukuo which, with the support of Mao Zedong and the other Chinese Communists, would reenter Korea and overthrow the Japanese government.

The period under the Japanese ascendancy shows a population with a strongly nationalist consciousness, but the extensive repressive measures in place prevented a single nationalist leader rising to the forefront of a Korean movement. There were several movements operating from abroad, and within the country, the student movement, the exiles in Soviet Russia, the exiles in China, the Righteous Army, the peasant movement, and the guerilla operations in Manchuria, but there was no single banner to unite and rally a population. As a result, the movement's effectiveness was severely limited under the Japanese occupation.

World War II

When World War II began in the Pacific in 1941, the Korean population was once again placed on war footing to support the Japanese effort. Half a million Koreans were forced into serving in the Japanese army. They did not receive equal treatment to the Japanese soldiers. The Japanese put their Korean soldiers in higher risk situations because they saw them as more expendable than their Japanese counterparts[xxii].

If war was tough on the Korean male population, it was outright torture for the female population. Some 200,000[xxiii] Korean women were forced into military brothels. Known as 'comfort women', these women were subjected to beatings, torture, and rape, and kept in conditions no better than most slaughterhouses[xxiv]. Many of the women never returned to their homes after the war. Many died during their ordeal, others died later due to the physical and psychological trauma they suffered, but also some refused to go home due to the intense feeling of shame. Today the Japanese government still refuse to acknowledge these 'comfort women' existed, despite the numerous accounts from survivors[xxv].

The Japanese Legacy

On 15 August 1945, the war ended. Japan surrendered to Allied forces and their 35-year occupation of the Korean peninsula came to an end. The Japanese left a divided Korean population with almost no middle class. A few Korean families who had collaborated with the Japanese had amassed a huge amount of wealth under the period of economic development, but the majority of the Korean population was left impoverished and without land. The blatant inequality between those who had collaborated with the Japanese and those who hadn't, left a population acutely sensitive to the injustices created under Japanese capitalism. In the wake of World War II, they hoped for an independent government which could address the issues of inequality and poverty.

Chapter 2 – A Korea Divided: The US Occupation of the South

During World War II, there was widespread uncertainty about what a post-war Korean peninsula would look like. The topic was first discussed at length on 23 November 1943 in Cairo at a meeting between Franklin D. Roosevelt and Chiang Kai-shek[xxvi]. The Chinese hoped that after the war, all Chinese territories seized by Japan would be returned to China, all islands in the Pacific under Japanese occupation would be removed from Japanese control and that Korea would receive its independence[xxvii]. Chiang Kai-shek wanted to see the Korean Provisional Government return to Korea from Shanghai and govern the country independently. Both Roosevelt and Chiang agreed to an independent Korea, but Roosevelt was concerned that any attempt to install the Provisional Government as the governing body in Korea would be seen as an attempt to exclude the Soviets and the Korean communists in exile in the Soviet Union. Roosevelt believed that a power struggle would be created in the region between the Chinese and Soviets which would only lead to more instability.

Although both parties agreed that an independent Korea should be established, neither knew how to bring it to fruition. The nature of the Korean independence movements operating in exile in other countries, meant that they were inherently dependent on foreign governments[xxviii]. The Provisional Government in China relied on funding from Chiang Kai-shek's Kuomintang (KMT) Government, and similarly, the movement in Irkutsk had relied on Soviet training and support. Once these movements re-entered Korea, they would need to prove themselves capable of representing the Korean population on the peninsula to unify support and form a stable government. There was no guarantee that either party would have the popularity necessary to achieve these aims.

Roosevelt was also unsure of the capacity of the Koreans to govern themselves after decades under Japanese rule. William R. Langdon, a foreign office official for the U.S. who spent time in Manchuria and Japan before

World War II, prepared a memo for the Roosevelt administration in 1942[xxix]. In it he argued that due to the extent of the Japanese occupation, Korea was in no position to effectively manage its own government. He recommended that Korea is guided by a larger power before it could be left to run independently. The memo mentioned the possibility of an international commission which could assist the Koreans until they had the capabilities of managing their own state independently.

Roosevelt had a post-war vision of a world regulated by the 'Big Four' powers: the United States, the Soviet Union, China and Great Britain. It was this vein of thought, which prompted him to adopt the idea of a North Pacific Regional Council which would administer Korea after the war. The council would be made up of the United States, China, and the Soviet Union[xxx]. He believed this would solve the issue of either China or the Soviet Union receiving preferential treatment on the peninsula after the war.

However, one thing concerned Roosevelt. He could not guarantee the Soviet Union would not enter the war in the Pacific. He feared Soviet troops would enter Manchuria to fight the Japanese armies in the Northern section of the Korean peninsula and would achieve a dominant position to occupy the entire Korean peninsula after the war[xxxi].

So, in September 1944, Roosevelt began taking steps to bring his Pacific Regional Council vision to fruition. The Supreme National Defense Council in Washington began working closely with the Chinese KMT government. Yang Yun-chu, director of the Department of East Asian Affairs in Chiang Kai-shek's government, was sent to Washington[xxxii] to draw up plans of an interim administration for a Korean government before it could be granted independence. However, despite conducting eleven meetings in January and February of 1945, little progress was made on clarifying how an international trusteeship would manage the administration. Both sides had differing ideas on the roles of the trusteeship and the length of time the interim government would need to be in power. The Chinese were under the impression Korea could be granted independence within five years, while the Americans had a much longer allied occupation period of around 25 to 30 years in mind[xxxiii].

When Roosevelt, Stalin, and Churchill met at Yalta in February of 1945, Roosevelt had the opportunity to bring Stalin on board with his vision of trusteeship for the Korean peninsula. He received an oral agreement[xxxiv] from Stalin that the United States, China, the USSR and perhaps Great Britain would have a hand in the administration of Korea once the war was over, but again there was little talk of the implementation of such a plan, or how it would function in practicality.

The end of the war and the division of Korea

The failure of the Roosevelt administration to make headway on any practical implementation or negotiation for the governance of Korea meant that when he died two months later, the US was back to square one under the Truman administration. Within a week of taking office, Truman had abandoned Roosevelt's idea of a joint trusteeship and begun searching for an alternative solution.

As the Russian agenda had become more expansionist in Europe and Red Army troops were gathering on the Chinese and Korean border, he saw the atomic bomb as a possible solution to the problem[xxxv]. He believed if he could guarantee the quick surrender of Japan by dropping an atomic bomb on a key city, the Soviet Union would have no need to enter the war in the Pacific and invade Manchuria and Korea. If the Soviets had no troops in the Korean peninsula when the Japanese surrendered, they would have no excuse to occupy any part of the peninsula.

On 6 August 1945, the United States dropped the first atomic bomb on Hiroshima, but Japan didn't surrender. Two days later, the Soviet Union declared war on Japan, much earlier than the U.S. planners predicted. The Red Army moved into North Korea to defeat the Japanese Kwangtung Army which was defending the north of the peninsula[xxxvi]. By the time the Japanese asked for surrender terms on 10 August, the day after the U.S. dropped the second bomb on Nagasaki, 250,000 Soviet troops accompanied by 35,000 Soviet-Koreans[xxxvii] had occupied several prominent cities in the north of Korea.

The Japanese military had divided Korea into the north, which was defended by the Kwangtung Army, and the south, which was defended by the Chosun Army. With the Kwangtung Army defeated and the Soviets in control of the north of the peninsula, Washington was desperately trying to prevent the complete annexation of Korea by the Soviet Union. The nearest American troops were 600 miles away in Okinawa[xxxviii]. So, late in the evening of 10 August, the Operations Division of the War Department in Washington were given 30 minutes to come up with a plan. Brigadier General George Lincoln had estimated that the Soviets could reach the 38th parallel before U.S. forces could land in the South and take Seoul. Based on this logic, this was the demarcation line proposed to the Soviets that evening. The plan was telegrammed to Stalin and, much to the surprise of the Joint Chiefs of Staff, he accepted it on 16 August[xxxix].

Soviet forces could have probably pushed further south before the U.S. military could have landed and secured Seoul, his decision to accept the U.S. proposal was surprising. It is believed that Stalin accepted the offer of demarcation at the 38th parallel to maintain a good working relationship with the allies in the post-war negotiations[xl]. His main goal was to secure the annexation of Eastern Europe and he believed that by conceding the South of the Korean peninsula to the Americans, he would be in a better position at the negotiating table for the European theatre and the decision on what to do with the rest of the seized Japanese territories. Stalin was also acutely aware of the left leanings of the Korean independence movements and was confident that Korea would remain pro-Soviet in the postwar era.

On 7 September, General Douglas MacArthur, the Supreme Allied Commander of the South West Pacific, formalized the agreement when he declared publicly to the Korean population the territory south of the 38 degrees north latitude were now under his military authority[xli].

The division of Korea had been completed. With no consultation or consideration of the wishes or desires of those inhabiting the peninsula, hasty decisions had been made by the Truman administration, with little forethought or understanding of the conditions within the country. The partition was initially established to provide a short-term solution to the problems which arose in the confusion of the Japanese surrender, yet today, the peninsula remains divided along the same demarcation line. With more forethought, planning and a step-by-step plan of the practical implementation of long-term goals, the U.S. under Truman could have avoided the short-term fix pitfalls which led to the deep divisions etched out in the country today.

Establishing the US occupation

If U.S. policy was confused and incoherent over the partition of the peninsula, policy on the day-to-day management of the country was nothing short of chaotic.

When U.S. forces arrived, they were shocked by the extent of the support of the radical left in the south of the country[xlii]. They quickly realized that most regions of the country had an active leftist movement and were not overly receptive to their American occupiers. The Korean population hoped for the installation of an independent government following the Japanese occupation. The idea of another military occupation did not appeal to them.l.

General Hodge was appointed military governor of South Korea by General MacArthur and immediately established a Korean Advisory Council in October of 1945. This would serve as an interim government until South Korea could undertake responsibility for its own governance as an independent country. Hodge wanted to bring in someone he could trust to lead the Korean Advisory Council. He needed a Korean, unsympathetic to communism, who had close ties to U.S. politicians and could be relied on to implement their policies across the south of the peninsula.

Syngman Rhee was the man chosen for the job. He was fiercely anti-communist and, over the 33 years he had been living in the US prior to the end of the war, he had built up strong connections within the US government. Rhee was initially flown to Tokyo in September, where he met with MacArthur, then he was sent to Seoul in mid-October[xliii]. Almost as soon as Rhee touched down in Korea, he was appointed President of the Independence Promotion Central Committee, Chairman of the Korean People's Representative Democratic Legislature and President of the Headquarters for Unification.

Unlike Roosevelt, Truman openly adopted a policy of containment toward communism. In December 1945, the Foreign Ministers of the U.S., Great Britain, and the Soviet Union met in Moscow at the Moscow conference to discuss the future of the Korean peninsula. When the details of an independent government couldn't be agreed upon, Truman abandoned the idea and adopted a policy of non-cooperation with the Soviet Union which sealed Korea's divided fate.

In 1946, he installed an interim legislature and interim government, led by Kim Kyu-shik and Syngman Rhee. The two institutions governed under the watchful eye of the U.S. Military Government. The U.S. chose to ignore the legitimacy claims of the Provisional Government operating in China due to its communist alignment. But the South Korean Interim Legislative Assembly encountered intense opposition across the country.

The installed government under Rhee and Kim failed to appeal to either the Korean left or right movements. The left movements ignored the legitimacy of the interim government and looked to the Provisional Government in exile as the sole administrative authority. Conservative groups also opposed the Interim Legislative Assembly. The Korean Democratic Party, who counted on the support of many of Korea's business owners and remained landowner classes, had none of their leaders selected to sit in the Legislative Assembly. Kim didn't command the popularity of the conservatives in the country and his appointment of the 45 members of the Legislative Assembly was comprised of mostly moderates like himself, who didn't appeal to conservative groups[xliv].

The interim government, under General Hodge's guidance, began an attempt to cleanse South Korea of leftist ideology. The Communist Party of Korea had changed its name to the Communist Party of South Korea and continued operating within the region. In November 1946, the influential communist group merged with the New People's Party of South Korea to create the Workers' Party of South Korea. The party had a significant following, active membership was around 360,000[xlv].

The U.S. Military Government immediately outlawed the party and launched a wave of left-wing repression. The Worker's Party of South Korea moved its operations underground and became clandestine by nature. They began to launch a guerilla struggle against the American Military Government. Although widespread persecution caused much of the party leadership to flee to the Soviet occupied north of the peninsula, they still enjoyed popularity in many regions of the south throughout the period of American military rule.

A Period of Turmoil

The U.S. Military didn't just have to contend with a left-leaning population. The arbitrary division of the peninsula along the 38th parallel had caused economic chaos. The heavy industries and plants which had transformed the Korean economy under the Japanese, were now predominantly located in the north, under Soviet control[xlvi]. According to a CIA Intelligence Memorandum from 1972, when the U.S. took South Korea in 1945, just 35%[xlvii] of the peninsula's heavy industry was established in the South.

The few industries located in the south, relied on electricity generated from the hydroelectric power plants on the Yalu River at the northernmost tip of the peninsula, which was also under Soviet control. Electricity produced in the south could only produce 9%[xlviii] of South Korea's electricity requirements.

Not only was the South plagued with electricity shortages, but the Japanese technicians and workers who had coordinated the day-to-day running of the factories and mines before and during the war, had returned to Japan[xlix]. The result was a South Korean economy without enough skilled workers and technicians to operate their few remaining factories and mines.

At the end of the war, the population in South Korea swelled as many Koreans returned from their periods of exile under the Japanese. Between 1945 and 1946, the population rocketed by 21%[i]. 1.8 million Koreans also entered the South from the Soviet occupied North between 1945 and 1950. This influx of refugees and returning exiles caused vast unemployment. In 1947, only half of the South Korean labor force was employed[ii].

Running out of options and unable to effectively manage the confusion in which South Korea had descended, the U.S. submitted the Korean issue to the UN. In September 1947, the UN General Assembly upheld Korea's claim to independence and began making preparations for an election to select an independent national legislative assembly. The Soviet Union refused to concede the North and it became clear the elections in 1948 would be for an independent government to govern the South alone.

As it became obvious to the public these elections would cement the division of the Korean peninsula, a series of protests erupted in Seoul and other major cities. The South Korean Worker's Party organized a general strike in protest of the separation from

February to March of 1948 and in April open rebellion broke out on the island of Cheju[lii]. On April 3rd, a group of rebels attacked police stations and government buildings on the island. They killed approximately 50 policemen in a display of discontent and defiance[liii]. The backlash was brutal. Prompted by the US Military Government, Rhee's administration embarked on a scorched earth campaign across Cheju, which left 60,000 civilians dead and the widespread destruction of island villages[liv]. Many of the details of Rhee's retribution against the rebels went unknown at the time. It was a Freedom of Information Act, filed many years later, that led to the information surrounding the crushing of the uprising coming to life.

In the run up to the election, other revolts broke out across South Korea. To pacify the left-leaning demonstrators, the U.S. government passed a bill providing a version of land reform and redistribution. However, when the reform was finally carried out in 1949, the benefits were largely confined to those loyal to the Rhee regime and most landless agricultural workers were left no better off.

Tthe elections went ahead in May 1948, with a follow-up election in July 1948. The South Korean Workers' Party boycotted the elections to avoid giving legitimacy to the process.

Syngman Rhee swept to victory in the sham elections with 92.3% of the popular vote and on 15 August 1948, the establishment of the Republic of Korea was formally declared for the regions South of the 38th parallel. By 29 June 1949, the United States Military had all been withdrawn except a handful of advisors[iv].

The U.S. occupation between 1945 and 1948 was a period of turmoil and confusion for the country. The lack of the U.S. understanding of the peninsula led to an arbitrary division along the 38th parallel and caused the inability of South Korea to manage a self-sufficient economy. There was no long-term strategy of what to do with Korea or how the U.S. would defend it. General Hodge received instructions to preserve stability, but had been stripped of almost every resource to do so by the agreed demarcation of the 38th parallel.

Truman's decision to adopt a stance of non-cooperation with the Soviet Union had created major uncertainty over the future of the peninsula and made it impossible to achieve a united, independent Korea at the end of the occupation. In 1947, with Chiang Kai-shek's government wobbling in China, and the Soviet dominance in the North, South Korea looked set to become the only region of Northeast Asia not under communist influence. The situation was precarious and many Americans in Washington were questioning their ability to defend South Korea.

Chapter 3 – The Forging of the North Korean State

The narrative that has been perpetrated in North Korean literature and propaganda surrounding the birth of the nation and the rise of Kim Il-sung describes a new proletariat seizing leadership under a national liberation movement led by Kim Il-sung himself. It portrays Kim as a righteous leader of a revolutionary Marxist-Leninist movement, fighting side-by-side with the Soviet forces in North Korea to overthrow the brutal Japanese occupiers[lvi].

In reality, Kim Il-sung's guerilla attacks against the Japanese in Manchuria were little more than a minor annoyance in the late 1930s and 1940s[lvii]. He was not a prominent leader of the communist movement prior to returning to North Korea during the Soviet invasion of 1945, and nor did the Korean people give him their support as soon as he returned to the peninsula. He had to work to obtain the leadership and it is unlikely he could have achieved it without significant Soviet support.

The Rise of Kim Il-sung

After the liberation of North Korea in August 1945, there were four political groups jockeying for power under the new Soviet occupation. There was the established domestic Communist group who had remained in Korea throughout the war, the Communists who had returned from exile in China who formed the Yenan faction, the Communists who had returned from Soviet Russia (including Kim Il-sung) and the non-Communist nationalists[lviii]. Initially, despite the Yenan faction's military training from Chiang Kai-shek's forces, and the Korean Russians having military experience in the Soviet Army[lix], it was the final group of non-Communists who enjoyed the most power.

As the Japanese fled North Korea in 1945, the governor of Pyongan Nando, the province in which the capital of Pyongyang is situated, transferred his power to the nationalists. Cho Man-sik, a non-Communist Christian teacher, was named the governor[lx] of the province. Once the Soviets took control, they appointed Cho as the chief of the Provisional Political

Committee, which governed over the whole Soviet occupied area.

Cho relied on his Christian power base for his support. There had been intense Christian missionary activities in Korea in the late 1800s which had led to the growth of a significant number of Christians in the region. Under the Japanese occupation, they had been persecuted for their reluctance to worship at the Shinto shrines. As a result, the Christian community in North Korea in 1945 was intensely politicised and had the potential to become a significant political force in the north of the peninsula[lxi]. In November 1945, Christian leaders united to form the Korean Democratic Party (KDP), *Choson Minjudang,* and established a government over the Soviet occupied North of the country.

Almost as soon as the Soviet Union had established a Provisional Political Committee, they began implementing Soviet economic reforms. Industries were brought under state control and lend reforms confiscated private property from landowners who had benefitted under Japanese rule.

However, this was a contentious issue for Cho's Provisional Political Committee. He was staunchly against the Soviet land reform programs and their grain purchase plans and therefore clashed with the Soviet authorities.

Without supporting the Soviet implemented reforms, Cho did not manage to stay in power for long. He was ultimately arrested by the Soviet command in 1946[lxii] for his non-compliance.

Almost as soon as Cho was arrested, sensing tides were turning, Christians began fleeing the north and entering the south. Between 1945 and 1951 between one and 1.4 million people[lxiii] fled North Korea, many of them Christians, due to the persecution by the Soviets and other Communist leaders. By April 1946, the KDP had relocated to Seoul[lxiv]. However, even after Cho's arrest and disposal, the Soviets kept the structure of the KDP to maintain the illusion of a democracy. They replaced Cho with a communist leader named Ch'oe Yong-gon.

Meanwhile, the competing communist factions were consolidating their power bases. The Yenan faction focused their attention on generating support among educated office workers with considerable results. Many bureaucrats who had worked under the Japanese joined the Yenan faction's Independence League. This allowed communist ideology to appeal to new demographics. Many Koreans who had remained in Korea throughout the Japanese occupation and the war, believed communism was for the poor classes and the uneducated.

The returning exiles from China persuaded the wealthier and more educated petty bourgeoisie that communism could be for them too[lxv].

Kim Il-sung, on the other hand, appealed to the poorer rural classes. His charismatic style of visiting factories and farms to offer "on the spot guidance" allowed him to build a strong power base among working people[lxvi]. His son and grandson, Kim Jong-il and Kim Jong-un, would both go on to use the same methods of generating support among the working classes, with both frequently photographed by North Korea state media on-site, inspecting a factory or construction project and smiling with the workers.

Throughout the 1940s, membership in the communist party rocketed to between 12% and 14% of the population[lxvii]. It offered poor, rural workers privileges and opportunities through political participation that had previously been out of their reach.

Kim Il-Sung had been working hard to ensure his followers of Soviet Koreans and those who had been in the Soviet Union during their years in exile were established at all levels of local and regional government[lxviii]. Kim was also helped by Soviet policy. The Soviets wanted to curb Chinese influence in North Korea, so they filled many of the media positions with Soviet Koreans[lxix]. With Kim's support from both the media and the poorer population and the Yenan faction's support among the urban educated class, the two communist groups were forced to outwardly work together to share their popular support[lxx].

In February 1946, the two groups would share leadership positions in the newly formed North Korean Provisional People's Committee. Kim-Il sung was named chairman, while the Yenan faction's Kim Tu-bong became vice-chairman. Once the two parties had successfully established a governing coalition, they agreed that the existence of two communist parties was damaging the country. The two factions agreed to merge and in July 1946 the newly formed North Korean Worker's Party (NKWP) held their first conference[lxxi].

As the South was having elections to establish an independent government, the North elected a Supreme People's Assembly in August 1948 which would govern the country. A new constitution was drawn up on 3 September and on the 9 September, Kim was sworn in as Premier of the newly formed Democratic People's Republic of Korea (DPRK). The Soviet Union declared Kim's government as the only lawful government on the peninsula shortly after and in December, the United Nations General Assembly responded by declaring the

Republic of Korea in the south as the only lawful government of Korea.

Coming together under one party allowed the NKWP to appeal to all segments of North Korean society. The party unified support and got their message out. The ultimate symbol of the success of their strategy and increased popularity came in June 1949. The North Korean Worker's Party joined up with the South Korean Workers Party[lxxii] to establish the Korean Worker's Party. It signified Kim's success in winning over the whole population, four years after entering Korea. By 1949, he had become a beacon for the Korean communist movement, in both the north and those being repressed, persecuted, and murdered in the south during the protests and rebellions. With Russian help, he had established himself as the leader of the North Korean people.

Chapter 4 –First Blood: The Outbreak of War

With Kim's position as leader of the Democratic Republic of Korea (DPRK) finally secure and the U.S. out of South Korea, he would turn his attention to his next goal: the reunification of the entire peninsula.

Communism was gaining momentum across the Asian continent. Communist ideology was spreading through China as Mao Zedong's revolution spread across the mainland, fueled by Soviet support and the retreat of Chiang-Kai Shek's nationalist government. Encouraged by the establishment of the DPRK, the insurgency movement was also still present in South Korea following the rebellions in the build-up to the election.

Kim sent a telegram to Stalin on 3 September in 1949. Kim knew that he would need extensive external support to undertake any military maneuver with the goal of unifying the peninsula. In the infamous telegram, he appealed to Stalin for "permission to begin military operations against the South[lxxiii]". The response from the Soviet Premier was clear in its response: "it is impossible[lxxiv]".

But within a year of Kim Il-sung's plea, North Korean forces would cross the 38th parallel and begin a military campaign against South Korean military forces. The conversations and meetings between Stalin, Kim Il-sung and Mao Zedong offer an insight into the U-turn in Stalin's decision and the events leading up to the mobilization of DPRK troops against the South.

Mao, Stalin, Kim Il-sung and the Movement towards War

The first time Kim's vision for the reunification of the Korean peninsula was discussed openly was during a meeting between Stalin and Kim in March of 1949[lxxv]. During the meeting, Stalin pledged to provide Kim's newly formed DPRK with economic aid, along with finances for railroad improvements and help for his Korean People's Army (KPA) in the form of aviation training for their forces[lxxvi]. Stalin was also careful to explicitly rule out any support Kim's goal of reunification[lxxvii].

This did not deter Kim Il-sung. He immediately began strengthening the KPA by looking to recruit Koreans living in the region of Manchuria in the north-east of China to expand the size of his army. He also sent the army's Chief Political Officer, Kim Il, to China to talk to Mao Zedong about the possibility of receiving Chinese military aid. The Chinese were more than happy to oblige. They saw a strong communist ally along the north-east border as a good way to strengthen their position in the region. They also saw it as an opportunity to reduce Soviet influence. If they could forge strong ties with North Korea, Mao believed China could become the new communist political power in the region. In this thinking, Mao promised the KPA two divisions of Sino-Korean soldiers currently stationed in Manchuria and pledged to return the Korean officers that were currently training within the Red Army by June[lxxviii]. Crucially, Mao also gave Kim the assurance he was looking for: "if a war breaks out between North and South Korea, we are also ready to give that is in our power"[lxxix].

With his encouragement from Mao's response, Kim sent Stalin that pleading telegram in September, but after Stalin's flat-out refusal to support an invasion of the South, Kim began to get restless. He wanted to strike while the iron was hot and he still had the support of the insurgency movement in the South.

In October, Chiang-Kai Shek's forces collapsed and fled mainland China to the island of Taiwan, signaling a likely victory for Mao and the Chinese Communists in mainland China. Mao formally declared the birth of the People's Republic of China (PRC) on 1 October. Although the Civil War was not over and Mao wanted to take Taiwan to complete his revolution, it changed the situation in the Asian theatre. As Mao's position looked more secure and his victory more guaranteed, Stalin and Mao's aims separated.

Mao remained set on taking Taiwan, but Stalin was vehemently against it. He believed a move against the island would prompt American military intervention that could lead to an all-out war between China, the USA and the Soviet Union. More importantly for Korea, he was concerned that once Mao took Taiwan, the U.S. would have no choice but to acknowledge the PRC internationally. He feared this would open the possibility of Sino-American diplomatic relations[lxxx] and the two nations would cooperate to curb the global influence of the Soviet Union.

His fears were justified. The Americans had devised their "wedge" diplomatic strategy which sought to provide to support for Chiang Kai-shek and the KMT in Taiwan, but simultaneously pursue a diplomatic relationship with Mao's Chinese Communist Party (CCP).

Kim hoped to capitalize on this period of uncertainty by taking the opportunity to appeal to Stalin once more for permission to begin military operations against the South. In January of 1950, Kim asked Stalin for another meeting to discuss reunification. He hinted to the Soviet Ambassador in North Korea, Terentii Shtykov, that Mao had already promised support and that Kim would look to Mao to provide what he needed if Stalin refused[lxxxi]. This was the encouragement Stalin needed. He did not want an invasion to go ahead without his approval and wanted to prevent any semblance of a mutual relationship developing between Kim and Mao that would erode the Soviet Union's regional influence. Stalin granted Kim's request for a meeting and invited him to Moscow to discuss the matter further[lxxxii].

Ahead of the meeting, Kim asked Stalin to provide North Korean aid credits for 1951 a year early to allow Kim to procure arms, ammunition and military equipment for the KPA. Stalin accepted and allowed Kim to offset the costs providing he could provide gold, silver, and monazite concrete for the Soviet nuclear program, which Kim obliged[lxxxiii].

At the end of March, Kim traveled to Moscow in a covert operation to keep the meeting a secret from Mao and the Chinese. He remained in Moscow until the middle of May[lxxxiv], where the two made plans for the DPRK's strike on the South. Their plans relied on a quick strike to catch the South unprepared, in conjunction with the military mobilization of South Korean communists loyal to Kim and North Korean guerrillas already positioned in the South of the peninsula.

Stalin was careful to add one condition to his acceptance of Kim's commencement of military activities against the South. He wanted Kim to talk to Mao first and get his support. Stalin agreed to Kim's plan but was nervous of the U.S. military coming to the aid of the South Korean forces. He told Kim Il-sung that if the United States joined the war, the Soviet Union would be unable to openly fight them[lxxxv]. He wanted Kim to get Mao's assurances the Chinese would provide support in the event that the U.S. army would enter the conflict in support of the Republic of Korea.

Stalin had skillfully maneuvered Kim's desire to unify the peninsula to work in favor of the

Soviet Union's political aims. He believed if he could get Chinese forces to fight the Americans, he would have succeeded in guaranteeing China's isolation from the Western powers[lxxxvi]. Leaving Mao's China diplomatically isolated was the only way Stalin could guarantee Chinese subordinacy to Soviet political strategy[lxxxvii]. It would also prevent Mao from devoting all his military forces to the campaign to take Taiwan and complete his revolution. If the war was a success, it would expand the buffer zones for Stalin's Soviet Union and be a serious dent to American influence. Cunningly, Stalin was orchestrating an open war against the U.S. without risking a single Soviet soldier.

Following Stalin's insistence that Kim gets Mao's committal, Kim secretly departed for Beijing on 13 May to meet Mao and Prime Minister, Zhou Enlai and sat down at the first meeting with the pair later that evening. Kim told them Stalin had pledged his support and successfully stoked Mao's fear Stalin wanted to support the reunification of North Korea before the campaign to take Taiwan. There is evidence Zhou Enlai clarified this with the Soviet Ambassador for Beijing and once Stalin himself had verified[lxxxviii] that he had given Kim's plan his approval, Mao quickly approved Kim's request for aid and assistance.

Mao likely agreed out of fear of upsetting Stalin. Mao desperately wanted Soviet Air support for his planned attack on Taiwan and didn't want to risk alienating the leader of the Soviet Union[lxxxix]. Mao believed that to deny Kim the support he wanted, and Stalin had asked for, would jeopardize Mao's future ability to negotiate support for his Taiwan offensive.

The sequence of meetings, telegrams, and conversations between the three heads of state show the decision to go to war arose out of Kim's insistence more than Stalin's ideas for Soviet expansion ideas. Stalin was initially against the idea, but once he explored ways to make the conflict work in favor of Soviet foreign policy objectives, he expertly manipulated Mao and the situation to become advantageous to him. It may have been Kim's initial idea, but the timing of the conflict ensured Stalin stood to gain the most from the conflict.

He prevented China from establishing diplomatic ties with the United States and prevented a Sino-North Korean military union which excluded the Soviet Union. He also pulled the United States into a war against a communist government, without the risk of Soviet lives on the front line. He had masterfully orchestrated Kim's dream to fulfill his vision.

Who Ignited the War?

Once Kim had Mao's pledge that the Chinese military would offer support to the KPA in their plan to reunify the peninsula, preparations were made for an invasion of the South. Although Kim had the intention of going to war, the western world view of an aggressive KPA charging across the 38th parallel against an unsuspecting and unprepared South Korean army fails to accurately consider all the forces at play in the conflict.

Before the outbreak of war on the 2 June 1950, there was much posturing from both sides of the 38th parallel. In 1950, Rhee's popularity began to wane and the government of the Republic of Korea looked more unstable than ever. The U.S. military insisted Rhee hold another general election in May. Rhee's party suffered huge losses, retaining just 22 seats out of 210[xc] and control over the county's General Assembly was handed over to a mixture of independent groups all competing for power.

Kim took this as an opportunity to rally support in the south for a single, united Korea. On 7 June, Kim and other leaders from the DPRK appealed to the population of South Korea to support the reunification of the entire peninsula through a free, nationwide election. He recommended that talks between the two governments take place in Haeju, a town in North Korea near the 38th parallel or Kaesung, a town in South Korea also near the 38th parallel[xci]. Kim deliberately called for Syngman Rhee to be excluded from the elections, hoping to play on his unpopularity to garner support among the southern population.

This made the situation more sensitive; the UN commission and U.S. military observers were deployed to monitor the 38th parallel. Four days later, on 11 June, three delegates were arrested for crossing the border into South Korea to appeal for reunification[xcii]. The situation was deemed so precarious that John Foster Dulles, a special consultant to the U.S. State Department, traveled to the Republic of Korea to inspect the situation.

On 19 June, Foster Dulles addressed the National Assembly, further pledging American support to South Korea and further increasing tensions across the peninsula.

Later that month, on 25 June, these tensions came to a head when the U.S. Ambassador to the Republic of Korea, Mr Muccio, reported the DPRK forces had crossed the 38th parallel[xciii]. A U.S. military observer report detailed how the South Korean forces were arranged for defense and the DPRK invasion caught the military by surprise[xciv]. Lt. Colonel Malonoy, acting Chief of Staff of the U.S. Military

Advisory Group, reported that by nightfall on 25 June all the southern territory west of the Imjin River was lost to DPRK forces to a depth of three miles[xcv], with the exception of the region in the Haeju province.

The DPRK undoubtedly crossed the 25th parallel and occupied the towns of Onjin and Kaesung on 25 June. However, the South Korean and American assertion they were unprepared for war and defend the North Korean attack doesn't account for the success of the South Korean counterattack on the North Korean town of Haeju. In a statement released which didn't receive anywhere near as much attention as the reports highlighting North Korean aggression, the South Korean army describes a successful counterattack on the town of Haeju on the morning of 25 June[xcvi].

Haeju had a population of around 82,000[xcvii] people and was the first railway junction above the 38th parallel which had a direct line to Pyongyang. The town would have had significant strategic interest for the South Korean army. It's connectivity to Pyongyang, just 65 miles away, would make it the ideal location from which to launch an invasion of the North Korean capital. Reports surrounding the outbreak of the conflict show that at around 4:00 am on 25 June, North Korean forces attacked the Onjin peninsula. A ground attack with four divisions, 70,000 men and 70 tanks followed around half an hour later[xcviii]. The assault had evidently been planned for quite some time as key locations along the 38th parallel were hit. At between 9.00 and 9.30 am, Kaesung, the most significant town taken by the KPA, fell into the communist's hands. However, an official broadcast from Seoul outlines the South Korean counter-attack entering Haeju at 9:00 am. This would mean the counterattack, took place before any significant towns in South Korea had fallen into the hands of the KPA.

Given the chronology, it is unlikely the South Korean forces were as unprepared as they portrayed themselves to be. General MacArthur would later submit a statement to the Joint Senate Committee Hearings outlining the level of preparedness of the South Korean forces for the outbreak of war. His statement shows t the South Korean forces were concentrated in one base between Seoul and the 38th parallel. This would also indicate the forces were not positioned to defend the 38th parallel as the U.S. has suggested, but were preparing for an invasion of their own, most likely on Haeju[xcix].

The war also suited Syngman Rhee's aims. In 1950, the Republic of Korea was becoming a tightly controlled police state under Syngman Rhee[c]. The more his popularity faded, the tighter he wanted to control the population. Political opponents were being jailed and inflation was rising. He was using the threat of an imminent North Korean attack as an excuse to defer the May elections by six months, a move that deeply concerned U.S. Secretary of State, Dean Acheson. The election only took place after Acheson threatened to review the aid package South Korea was receiving if elections were not held[ci].

Rhee also made no secret of the fact he wanted to invade the North to achieve reunification. Throughout 1950, he made several provocative speeches which hinted at the use of military force against North Korea, the most significant of which came on 1 March when he referred to Kim's government as "foreign puppets"[cii]. In this regard, it is entirely plausible that Rhee would give the command for a South Korean invasion, or at the very least, wish to provoke Kim into striking so he could use the attack as an excuse to occupy Haeju.

Regardless of who occupied the first town, on 27 June the U.S. appealed to the UN Security Council to give its approval to intervene in the war against North Korean aggression under the banner of the United Nations. Because the People's Republic of China had yet to be recognized by the UN, and the Soviet Union were boycotting the Security Council in protest at the decision, the UN Resolution was passed without the input or vetoes of the Soviet Union and the PRC. The Council passed Resolution 83, which determined the aggression shown by North Korea to be a breach of the peace on the peninsula and ordered them to cease hostilities or a military force to restore peace would be deployed.

On receiving the UN's blessing, Truman ordered the U.S. Air Force to provide assistance to South Korean forces. Like Stalin, Truman was also able to manipulate the situation to serve his interests. On 27 June, he also moved the 7th Fleet to contain Taiwan and prevent the PRC of completing their revolution[ciii]. Truman had wanted an excuse to openly provide military assistance to Chiang Kai-shek's KMT government in exile and this demonstration of communist aggression had been the perfect guise.

Undoubtedly the war occurred on 25 June because the North Korean army crossed the 38th parallel but given the convenience of war for all parties involved, it could just have easily occurred from an invasion of Haeju in the coming weeks by South Korean forces. The war benefitted Stalin's aims, Kim's aims, Rhee's alms, and ultimately Truman also seized the opportunity to gain influence over Taiwan and pledge military support for the

KPA. No player involved was in a position to uphold peace, ensuring the precarious curtain of peace along the 38th parallel came crashing down and plunging the peninsula into open warfare.

Chapter 5 – Strike Hard and Strike Fast: The US Retreat

Truman's decision to militarily intervene on the Korean peninsula represents a distinct change in U.S. strategy. American forces had withdrawn from the peninsula and despite outwardly pledging aid and support, they did not have troops stationed in the Republic of Korea before Truman made the decision to commit U.S. ground forces.

The Republic of Korea Army in Retreat

In the days following the North Korean invasion, the situation in the Republic of Korea went from bad to outright chaotic. In the five days in between crossing the 38th parallel and the arrival of the United States military to support the South Korean government, Syngman Rhee fled Seoul in his special train and moved the entire Republic of Korean Army (ROKA) headquarters to the South of the city. In doing so, he panicked the civilian population in Seoul and left troops fighting north of Seoul without any communication to their superiors and the rest of the ROKA. Unsurprisingly, the forces defending the South Korean capital began surrendering and retreating and before long the KPA had taken most of the capital and the front line had moved below Seoul. Rhee would stop his train at Taejon to promise the troops he would stay and fight to the death, before hopping back on his train and heading for Mokpo, then on to Pusan, well within the secure Pusan perimeter. With a leader interested in only saving himself, it is little wonder the Republic of Korea Army had little appetite to risk their lives in battle. ROKA forces were surrendering in huge numbers, often fleeing the battlefield without their weapons and supplies.

After the U.S. had UN authorization to restore peace on the peninsula with military force, Truman and MacArthur needed to make the decision of what capacity they would be involved in defense of South Korea. They wanted to preserve the government in South Korea, but were wary of Soviet military intervention on the peninsula. Many in the

Truman administration were against the use of ground forces because they believed it would instigate the Soviet Union to also deploy troops in Korea, thus entangling the two superpowers in open warfare. The National Security Council met on 28 June and discussed the possibility of Soviet military intervention on the peninsula. They concluded if Soviet troops entered the conflict to assist the North Korean forces, "United States forces should defend themselves, should take no action to aggravate the situation and should report the situation to Washington[civ]".

Later that day, John H. Church, Head of the survey team in South Korea, told General MacArthur the only way South Korea could prevent the collapse of the government and total communist annexation would be with American intervention[cv]. This prompted yet more concern from the Truman administration. But on the afternoon of 29 June, the American Government got the reassurance they were searching for. Washington received word from Moscow that the Soviet Union had no intention of committing ground forces to assist the KPA[cvi].

This was a tipping point for Truman, who felt reassured he could commit troops to Korea without worrying about military escalation from the Soviet Union. Acheson was also calmed and began to push for the commitment of American ground forces to uphold South Korean independence[cvii]. Truman was still cautious and didn't want to commit any more forces than he needed to. He suspected, quite rightly, the Russians were hoping the Chinese would do their fighting for them[cviii] and didn't want to provoke China into entering the war either.

On the evening 29 June, Truman was ready to give his instructions. He ordered the deployment of air and naval forces to secure the Fusan-Chinhae area, which would become to be known as the Pusan perimeter, in the southeastern corner of the peninsula. He deployed the air force to bomb targets, including those north of the 38th parallel, providing the air force avoided targets north, in the border regions to avoid provoking Chinese or Soviet intervention[cix].

The following day, MacArthur reported back from Korea with his recommendations. He wanted a Regimental Combat Team, along with two divisions of troops to carry out Truman's aims of securing South Korea and restoring the 38th parallel as the natural demarcation line. Truman was disappointed. He had hoped that ground forces wouldn't be necessary; however, he did concede to MacArthur's recommendations and made arrangements on 30 June for American troops to be deployed to South Korea.

Truman's Decision for American Intervention

Truman's decision to commit ground troops to Korea would shape American foreign policy throughout the Cold War period. It represented a new stance towards the Soviet Union.

In 1949, the Soviet Union developed the atom bomb. It became even more imperative for Truman and subsequent administrations to avoid a direct conflict with the Soviet Union out of fear it would escalate into a nuclear conflict.

Following the conflicts in Greece and Turkey, where American funding had attempted to prevent the spread of communism, Truman was determined Korea could not be engulfed by communism and fuel Soviet expansionist fires. He believed the invasion from the Kim Il-Sung's forces was a manifestation of Soviet expansionist ideals[cx] and the best way to prevent a future war with the Soviet Union, would be to openly fight communism with ground troops in the Asian theatre, in the hope that a communist defeat there would cause Stalin to reel in his expansionist ideas. Truman therefore wanted to provide support the French colonial forces in Vietnam and secure Taiwan to prevent any further spread of communism. This dogged insistence that communism should not spread in Asia would lead to the deployment of ground troops first in Korea and years later in Vietnam.

The political situation at home had also changed. Joseph McCarthy, the dogged senator for Wisconsin, had begun his campaign of doggedly rooting out communist sympathizers. After the trial of Algar Hiss, a top government official, over allegations of being a Soviet Spy in 1948[cxi], Truman felt he needed to prove his strength against communism to the electorate at home. If he allowed South Korea, a state occupied by the U.S. just two years previously, to fall into the hands of communism, he would have to face difficult questions from McCarthy's band of supporters and the U.S. population at large.

Truman drew his red lines and made the decision, in what would be one of the defining decisions to shape the geopolitics of the 21st century and tie the United States to two bloody and drawn out wars in Asia.

An Enemy Underestimated

With the Republic of Korea Army in full retreat, the American forces arrived in Korea unprepared for the effective, highly organized fighting of the KPA. MacArthur's initial request for two divisions was extended to 30,000 troops less than a week later. A week after that he asked for eight divisions in total[cxii]. The

North Koreans had severely surpassed the expectations of the American forces. They were an effective fighting force, skilled in the art of guerilla warfare, with women among their ranks and plenty of sympathizers in the south. The military editor of *the New York Times*, Hanson Baldwin summed them up when he called them "as trained, as relentless, as reckless of life, and as skilled in the tactics of the kind of war they fight as the hordes of Genghis Khan.[cxiii]"

With no previous experience against this kind of warfare, the U.S. forces had little idea of how to defeat them. They adopted a strategy of razing suspected communist villages to the ground. Towns and villages suspected of harboring communists had their civilian population removed and interned on the islands off the coast of Pusan, forbidden to return. Their homes were destroyed and the town or village totally destroyed[cxiv]. The city of Sunchon had 90% of its population arrested, while Yechon had every single civilian removed[cxv].

Truman continued to commit American troops to quell the North Korean momentum. By the end of July, there were 47,000 Americans fighting alongside 45,000 South Koreans against just 70,000 North Koreans, but the retreat still continued[cxvi]. It wasn't until the 1st Marine Brigade was deployed in August the retreat eventually slowed and front lines were established.

With the retreat finally curbed, the American and Republic of Korean command took stock of the situation. They had been pushed back to an 80x50 mile area in the southeastern tip of the peninsula, running from Pohang, to Taegu, then on to the Chinju-Masan coastal region. There were 98,000 KPA troops in the south of the peninsula. The South Korean capital, Seoul, was in North Korean hands, while half of the ROK forces lay dead, had been captured, or were declared missing. Around 70% of the Republic of Korea Army had lost their weapons in their hurry to retreat from the battlefield and only two divisions remained at full fighting capability[cxvii].

Kim Il-sung's plan he had hatched with Stalin during the meeting the previous march had set out to strike the ROK hard and fast to unify the peninsula quickly, and he nearly succeeded. He had forced MacArthur to play his hand and by 8 September every available combat troop was fighting in North Korea except the 82nd Airborne Division, a far cry from the two divisions that MacArthur had initially believed would send the KPA running for the 38th parallel. 83,000 U.S. troops coupled with 57,000 ROK and British reinforcements[cxviii] were needed to halt the

North Korean advance, but it had come at a cost.

In the closing days of August, the KPA launched another offensive to break the U.S. and ROK lines. Three KPA battalions crossed the Naktong River and took Pohang and Chinju. The U.S. forces were forced to relocate the headquarters to Pusan[cxix]. These two weeks saw some of the bloodiest fighting of the war and by the middle of September, there were long casualty lists.

Between 25 June, when the war began, and 15 September, there were more than 20,000 American soldiers injured and 4,280 dead[cxx]. These losses paled in comparison to the losses taken in the Republic of Korea Army. During the war for the South, 111,000 South Koreans were killed with more than 106,000 wounded and 57,000 still missing. For those who survived, many were homeless as 314,000 homes had been destroyed[cxxi].

The U.S. and ROK forces had been humiliated on the world stage. The United States had defeated two of the greatest armies on the planet in the Japanese and the Germans, and now a newly formed communist army had pushed them back to a small pocket of space on the southeast corner of the peninsula. It had taken almost their entire military force just to prevent the total seizure of Korea by the advancing communists and their position still didn't look secure. But MacArthur had a plan to restore U.S. pride and turn the tides of the Korean War.

Chapter 6 – Bittersweet Victories: American Revival and China's Decision to Cross the Yalu

MacArthur's ambitious master plan turned the tide of the war and turned the Korean conflict on its head. U.S. and ROK forces went from being pinned down in the Pusan perimeter, with the sea at their backs and the waves of North Korean onslaught crashing into their front, to recapturing Seoul and re-establishing the 38th parallel in just a couple of weeks.

Forming MacArthur's Legacy

Credit for the spectacular revival of U.S. forces can only be laid at the feet of one man,

General Douglas MacArthur. MacArthur had been planning what would be his crowning legacy since 29 June, when he took a flight to Suwon in the early days of the war. Amidst the panic and retreat of the South Korean Army and civilians, he formulated the idea of orchestrating an amphibious landing near Seoul[cxxii] to cut North Korean supply lines, retake the capital and isolate KPA troops in the South, which could then be rounded up and crushed. He decided that Inchon would be the perfect place for such a landing.

Almost immediately MacArthur ordered his advisors to begin the planning of "Operation Blueheart". However, as North Korean troops pushed forward with alarming force, the plan was put on hold while American lines were reorganized and more troops were brought in to halt the advance.

The plan for an amphibious landing was soon revived under "Operation Chromite"[cxxiii], with Inchon as the target and 15 September set as the execution date. But the plan was not without its opponents. Senior Admirals and Marine Generals were skeptical. Inchon could only be accessed by a narrow corridor and the whole corridor could be defended by the deployment of North Korean guns and artillery on Wolmi Island. Inchon also had unpredictable and extreme tides. The height difference between low and high tide was as much as ten meters. If the landing was not timed to perfection, the landing crafts became stuck as soon as the tide went out. With so many uncertainties, many of the Generals and Admirals were unwilling to take men away from the fierce defense of the Pusan perimeter to embark on such an ambitious and potentially dangerous amphibious offensive[cxxiv].

It took all of MacArthur's guile and oratory skills to persuade the Generals of his plan. On 23 August, he met with senior admirals, generals and army and navy chiefs of staff in Tokyo to hear their grievances. After listening intently to their concerns while smoking his pipe, he stood to address them and sooth their discontent. What followed was a passionate 45minute address that would decide the fate and legacy of not only MacArthur himself, but of the whole American intervention in Korea. He outlined his arguments for the landing, concluding with the rousing words, "I can almost hear the ticking of the second hand of destiny. We must act now or we will die. Inchon will succeed, and we will save 100,000 lives. We shall land at Inchon, and I will crush them[cxxv]".

The Inchon Landing

MacArthur's words could not have been more prophetic. On 10 September, the prelude for the landing began. British and American cruisers and warplanes began the bombardment of Wolmi Island, disabling much of the KPA's weaponry and paving the way for the 260 landing ships to land at Inchon five days later[cxxvi].

To orchestrate the landing at Inchon, MacArthur recruited the amphibious mastermind behind the successful Leyte landing in the Philippines and the Omaha Beach landing in Normandy during World War II, Admiral Arthur Dewey Struble[cxxvii]. He navigated a perfectly timed landing between the shifting bays and tides. Kim had failed to mine the port and had as little as 2,000 KPA troops positioned there. They were powerless to resist the invasion and the marines landed with minimal opposition[cxxviii].

The landing was executed to perfection, a welcome scrap of good news coming from the conflict after weeks of American and South Korean losses dominating the headlines.

Kim Il-sung was forewarned about the landing by Mao and the Chinese, but was powerless to prevent the success of the American landing force. When the retreat slowed and American troops dug in around Pusan in the Southeast, Zhou Enlai ordered the General Staff of the People's Liberation Army (PLA), Lei Yingfu, to draw up a forecast of likely future American movements. Lei concluded the U.S. would likely attempt an amphibious landing and Inchon would probably be the site[cxxix]. On the same day as MacArthur was rousing his generals with his speech in Tokyo, Lei briefed Mao about his suspicions, who relayed the information to Kim Il-sung. Kim's Russian advisers were also feeding him similar warnings. For reasons, unknown Kim didn't act on them, to his own loss.

The Intelligent Retreat

Within two weeks of the landing at Inchon, American forces had retaken Seoul and North Korean troops were fleeing to the North across the mountains[cxxx]. By early October U.S. forces had restored the 38th parallel divide and had succeeded in containing the spread of communism on the peninsula.

Had the Americans stopped there, the conflict could have been ended. The 38th parallel would have been recognized and restored and Truman could celebrate the successful completion of his pre-war objectives. He had succeeded at avoiding open conflict between U.S. troops and Chinese or Soviet forces, without allowing the Republic of Korea to fall to communism. The establishment of the pre-June demarcation lines at the end of September could have saved thousands of

American, North Korean and Chinese lives. However, this was not to be.

On 9 September, six days before the Inchon landing, the National Security Council issued document number 81, advising the President on his course of action once the 38th parallel had been re-established[cxxxi]. The report concluded that the restoration of forces to the 38th parallel, as they were on 25 June, would not be desirable to the U.S. It recommended Truman push forward with the reunification of the whole Korean peninsula by military force in North Korea[cxxxii].

Truman agreed and authorized the use of American military force above the 38th parallel, although he did add the stipulation that only the Republic of Korea Army should be involved in operations near the Manchurian border and if there was any sign of Soviet aggression it should be reported immediately and U.S. troops assume defensive positions[cxxxiii].

Despite recognizing the North Korean decision to cross the 38th parallel on 25 June as a clear act of communist aggression, the U.S. Security Council would see little problem with U.S. forces doing precisely the same thing a little over two months later. So, U.S. forces embarked on a military campaign north of the 38th parallel to unify the peninsula under ROK rule. MacArthur split his force into two columns[cxxxiv] with the intention of forming a pincer movement and trapping the remaining KPA troops against the Yalu River in the middle of the two columns before closing in on them and crushing them.

In early October, the North Korean forces were in full retreat, although unbeknownst to MacArthur and Truman, unlike the frantic retreat of the ROK forces earlier in the summer, this was a calculated and intelligent retreat.

Recovered notes from the notebook of Pak Ki-song, the KPA 8th division Chief of Political Intelligence, show the KPA had a plan of their own. They wanted to lure the Americans deep into North Korean territory, towards the Yalu River to spread the U.S. forces thinly over a vast area and ever closer to the Chinese border[cxxxv].

China Crosses the Yalu

As the U.S. forces pursued the KPA deeper into North Korea towards the end of September and early October, American Intelligence agencies considered the possibility that China would enter the war in support of Kim Il-sung's government.

On 20 September the CIA discussed the possibility that Chinese "volunteers" may come to the aid of the KPA but concluded that, like Stalin, Mao had no interest in engaging his Chinese forces in open conflict with the U.S. forces[cxxxvi]. Even as late as 24 November, just days before the Chinese offensive as MacArthur's forces marched on the Yalu River, the CIA still didn't suspect the impending Chinese intervention. But why was the U.S. so convinced a Chinese offensive was so out of the question?

Internally, China's economy was shattered after Mao's revolution[cxxxvii]. Inflation was high and with Mao's attention on an assault on Taiwan, the U.S. policymakers did not consider North Korea to be high on Mao's list of priorities.

The U.S. also placed too much faith in the Soviet policy of non-intervention. They wrongly assumed the Chinese would take their lead from the Soviets on the matter and presumed that Stalin's decision not to provide support and assistance automatically extended to Mao[cxxxviii].

There was some logic to this. The Sino-Soviet relationship in 1950 saw each country maintain their own sphere of influence. The Soviet Union provided weapons and support for Kim Il-sung in North Korea, while the Chinese provided aid and support to Ho Chi Minh and his communist forces in Vietnam.

The Truman administration placed too much emphasis on these spheres and assumed that there would be no crossover in support, especially as the Vietnamese communists were planning an assault on the French colonialists in Vietnam at the time and would need all the Chinese support they could get[cxxxix].

The decision to commit Chinese forces if the North Korea was overrun had already been decided during Kim Il-sung's visit to Beijing before the outbreak of war. On 4 August, just a couple of weeks after the start of the war, Mao already had Chinese military advisors in Pyongyang reporting back on the Korean war situation[cxl]. It was decided in late September, after the American successes at Inchon, that Chinese forces would enter the war. The only thing that remained to be decided was when and how large the force would be. On 30 September, Mao told Stalin he would send 12 infantry divisions to North Korea but Stalin was concerned that such a large display of force would cause an escalation of the conflict[cxli]. In the end Mao would commit these divisions against Stalin's wishes.

The Truman Administration failed to fully consider China's situation in its analysis. While the U.S. forces were not a direct threat to Mao's national security, the prospect of a U.S. occupied North Korea would pose Mao considerable issues in the future. China needed to garrison troops along the Manchurian border to maintain a line of defense against their U.S.-occupied neighbors. The Northeastern region of China housed much of the country's heavy industry and was incredibly valuable to Mao. Manchuria was home to China's steel and coal industries and the hydroelectric power plants on the Yalu which provided electricity. The 1,000km border needed a substantial number of troops to protect it, meaning higher costs and fewer troops available for the future assault of Taiwan[cxlii]. He also feared that with a U.S. occupied neighbor, it would fuel the anti-communist elements present in China who were against his policies. He couldn't afford to allow the anti-communist groups to gain momentum so shortly after the communist revolution and decided that intervention now to prevent the entire U.S. takeover of the peninsula, would save China money and troops in the long term and help Mao create a more politically stable Chinese Communist Government.

The Truman Administration also failed to consider the extent of Sino-Korean cooperation during the Chinese Civil War. The Korean Provincial Government had been established in Shanghai during the U.S.occupation of the South and many

Koreans had fought for the Chinese Communist Party (CCP) during the Civil War[cxliii]. This assistance had not gone unnoticed by Mao, who was happy to assist the Korean communists in the Civil War of their own.

There were also warning signs which went unnoticed. In the middle of November, the CIA noticed the North Korean retreat didn't resemble the normal retreat of an army in flight. MacArthur's pincers met limited resistance from KPA troops, even as they took Chongjin and Kim Il-sung's heartland, Kapsan. The CIA began to suspect the retreat was a ploy to launch a counter-offensive. Reconnaissance pilots also reported sightings of large numbers of troops gathering in the countryside towards the Manchurian border[cxliv], but there was limited consensus among the intelligence agencies and MacArthur's forces continued to push forward and stretch their supply lines as the bitter Korean winter approached.

There were signs on the ground that should have caused alarm bells for Truman. Among the captured KPA prisoners of war there were Chinese troops from six different Chinese Armies, a clear indication of significant Sino-Korean cooperation[cxlv]. The Chinese launched a small, bloody offensive across the Yalu at the end of October[cxlvi], hoping that their mere presence would deter the March towards the Chinese border and cause MacArthur to return to the 38th parallel. They attacked and then vanished. But MacArthur was relentless in his push onwards.

Internally, Zhou Enlai was condemning the American crossing of the 38th parallel as a direct threat to Chinese national security[cxlvii]. This, along with the small offensive at the end of October was as much a message to the Chinese population as it was to the Americans. Zhou and Mao needed to create the right political context to intervene in the Korean conflict. War with the American forces would be expensive and mean sacrifices for the Chinese civilian population. Framing the war as a response to American aggression and a purely defensive measure allowed them to sell the war to the Chinese population[cxlviii]. This also suited Kim. He wanted to wait for the opportune moment for Chinese intervention, once the American lines had been sufficiently stretched and a counter offensive would do the most damage.

The Chinese Strike

The Chinese counter offensive began in earnest on 27 November 1950. As planned, the American forces were thinly stretched across North Korea and the brutal Chinese attack cut the allied forces down. The 1st

Marine Division found themselves pinned down at the Changjin Reservoir[cxlix] and once again, the ROKA forces almost entirely collapsed.

On 4 December, the Truman Administration changed MacArthur's brief, making the preservation of the United States forces the new primary objective. With such overexposure and stretched lines, the U.S. forces could do nothing except concentrate on survival. By 6 December, Pyongyang had returned to North Korean control and the following day, the new front line was just 20 miles north of the 38th parallel[cl], unraveling all the allied advances of the previous six weeks.

The counter offensive had decimated ROK and U.S. forces. The U.S. suffered 335,000 casualties[cli] in some of the war's most intense fighting. MacArthur was furious and called the Chinese offensive "one of the most offensive acts of international lawlessness of historical record.[clii]" He ordered the complete aerial destruction of North Korea from the Manchurian border southwards in retaliation. Entire villages were engulfed in flames as the North Korean countryside was bombarded with napalm and American ordnance.

It took Truman threatening to deploy atomic weapons at a news conference on 30 November to halt the Chinese advance. It was the ominous threat of atomic destruction and the shrewd battlefield tactics of General Matthew Ridgway that halted the Chinese advance just south of Seoul.

In one swoop, Chinese forces had eradicated U.S. forces from the North of the peninsula and retaken Seoul for the Korean communists. The successes of MacArthur's Inchon landing had almost all been nullified by Chinese intervention. If MacArthur can take the blame for much of the U.S. successes at Inchon, he and Truman must also take the blame for the catastrophic loss of life caused by the Chinese Army. Warning signs of an impending Chinese invasion were ignored and intelligence reports failed to convince MacArthur or Truman to stop the American advance. American forces had gone from celebrating their Inchon victory, to scurrying south to lick their wounds. With the Truman administration looking for blame to be allocated, MacArthur would find himself with a target on his back.

Chapter 7 – How Do You Solve a Problem Like China?

Once again, the tide of the Korean War had shifted. By the end of January, Ridgway was in the position to lead forces back towards Seoul to reclaim the capital. After weeks of tough fighting, American forces retook Seoul and in the Spring of 1951 the battle lines hardened and stabilized along similar lines to those that still scar the peninsula today.

The Fall of Douglas MacArthur

With the battlefield more or less stabilized, Truman faced the next big decision of his presidency. How would he deal with the intervention of China in the Korean conflict? MacArthur's position was unambiguous. He called for the carpet bombing of North Korea and China and demanded that the air war is brought against Chinese targets. He also wanted to bring Chiang Kai-shek's forces into Korea from Taiwan and use them against the Chinese, thereby widening the scope of the war, increasing the troop numbers on the peninsula and further dragging American forces into the Korean quagmire.

Truman was now skeptical of MacArthur's judgment. He had met Truman in October, just a month before China's offensive and assured him the chances of a Chinese intervention were slim. He had been proven wrong once, it was highly possible he would be proven wrong again.

In a move which shocked the nation, Truman announced the firing of MacArthur on 11 April 1951. The public was initially against the firing and received MacArthur with a hero's welcome on his return. There were even rumblings of him making a run as a presidential candidate in the upcoming 1952 Presidential Election, but it never materialized[cliii].

The firing caused a very public argument between Truman and MacArthur, each representing opposing views on how to handle Chinese aggression in Korea. MacArthur advocated the side of unlimited warfare, while Truman on the other hand, wanted to keep the Korean War limited in scope. He didn't want a wider war in Asia, he believed the European theatre was far more important to the outcome of the Cold War[cliv] and he accused MacArthur of insubordination and being unable to see the bigger picture. He also desperately wanted to avoid any provocation which would lead to Soviet intervention and potentially trigger a third world war.

Despite the public opinion at the time, Truman had very good reasons for his firing of Douglas MacArthur. However, these valid reasons went unreported to the public and had little effect on MacArthur's high popularity at the time. In the 1970s, secret testimonies which took place in the Senate Hearings after MacArthur's firing revealed the true failings of MacArthur's proposed Korea solutions. They exonerate Truman's decision somewhat and offer the reader a glimpse of what a MacArthur driven Korean policy would look like.

The Joint Chiefs of Staff (JCS) who heard the Senate Hearings were utterly unconvinced by MacArthur's calls to widen the war. Omar Bradley, the Chairman of the JCS and a military man himself, condemned MacArthur's strategy as putting the U.S. in "the wrong war, in the wrong place, at the wrong time and with the wrong enemy[clv]".

A look at the military situation in Korea in the winter and spring of 1950 and 1951 shows why MacArthur's strategy was misguided. There were 35 active Soviet divisions in the

Far East, consisting of around 500,000 troops and 85 submarines in total[clvi]. Should the Russian force be mobilized against the American enemy, it would be impossible to get supplies from the American bases in Japan to the Korean peninsula past the Soviet submarines and AirForce. Should the ground force of half a million troops enter the peninsula, it would have been impossible to evacuate the American troops already in Korea.

While the U.S. was pinned down in Korea at the 38th parallel, there was no reason for these Soviet forces to intervene; however, if the bombing campaign was extended into China, or the U.S. forces gained the upper hand and pushed the Chinese back to Manchuria, there were no guarantees the Soviets would not enter the conflict. After the Chinese took them by surprise with their entry into the conflict, the U.S. government no longer had any confidence in Stalin's pledge to stay out of Korea.

The other issue with MacArthur's call for an extension of the war, was that the U.S. had very few forces to escalate the war with. According to Hoyt Vandenberg, the chief of staff of the Air Force, 80-85%[clvii] of the Air Force was already in Korea. Aside from the decision to bomb Chinese targets potentially causing an escalation of the theatre of war, it would also stretch the capabilities of the U.S. Air Force at the time. Vandenberg would never disclose this publicly, but in the Senate Hearings following the removal of MacArthur, he called the U.S. Air Force a "shoestring force"[clviii].

One of the other grievances MacArthur had with Truman's decision to maintain a limited war was he believed the Chinese were operating at their unlimited, full battle capacity and Truman's decision to limit the war was tying American hands and causing unnecessary loss of American life[clix]. Evidence also shows him to be incorrect on this front too. It was precisely China's decision to limit their forces that led to the preservation of more American life. The Chinese had 26 aviation divisions available during the Korean War[clx], yet they had not used their air capabilities against the U.S. ground forces or communication lines. If the U.S. extended their air war into China, the Chinese would undoubtedly retaliate by escalating their own war in the air, and most likely with Soviet air support. This would most likely nullify any advantages gained from the bombing of Chinese targets[clxi]. In reality, it is highly likely that in maintaining a limited war, conditions actually favored the Americans, as they used their aerial capabilities across North Korea while the Chinese didn't fully utilize theirs.

This view was echoed by the Army Chief of Staff, J. Lawton Collins. When MacArthur first advocated the bombing of China, American ground forces were spread out thinly across North Korea[clxii]. Should the Chinese have bombed them then, the tenth corps would have been cut off at Hungnam and any operation to evacuate them would have been difficult under Chinese and Soviet aerial bombardment.

MacArthur's final strategy was the appeal to bring the Chinese Nationalist Army from Taiwan to confront the Chinese communists in North Korea. The Senate Hearing was also skeptical of this decision. The Chinese Nationalists had already fallen to the Chinese communists once during the Chinese Civil War, why would their fate be any different fighting in a foreign country with no public support? The Senate Hearing concluded that any use of the Chinese Nationalists in Korea would weaken the U.S. position, not strengthen it. Omar Bradley said of Chiang Kai-shek's forces, "their leadership is poor, their equipment is poor, and their training is poor[clxiii]". They would have offered little in the way of an advantage to the much better trained American forces already fighting on the peninsula.

There was one more reason for Truman's decision to remove MacArthur. This hinged on

Truman's ability to trust MacArthur in a situation where the U.S. might resort to atomic weapons. In March 1951, MacArthur asked Truman for full atomic authorization to maintain American supremacy in the Korean War[clxiv]. The JCS were also considering the use of atomic weapons should the Chinese commit significantly more troops to the conflict and push the allied forces back down towards Pusan, as they had the previous summer. Truman even came as close as to order the transfer of the Mark IV atomic bombs to military custody on 6 April[clxv], but luckily the Chinese did not choose to reinforce their numbers. With MacArthur's hawkish approach to the war and thirst for escalation, Truman knew that if atomic weapons were to be deployed, he would want a general that he could trust to exert extreme caution and tact. MacArthur was not that general.

Exploring the implications of MacArthur's Korean strategy shows it would have undoubtedly led to a further loss of American life, escalation of the war and, potentially, mutually assured destruction in the form of a WWIII scenario. Although unpopular at the time, hindsight and declassified documents surrounding the follow-up Senate Hearings show Truman's tact and intelligence in replacing MacArthur as the head of allied forces. He replaced him with Matthew Ridgway who had demonstrated himself on the battlefield after leading the campaign to retake Seoul, and Truman saw him as being much more aligned with his own strategy for Korea. He was also a much safer option in the event of the deployment of atomic weapons, a prospect which lay on the table throughout the following ceasefire negotiations.

With that, MacArthur, the once lauded war hero, was removed from command. The man who had almost single handedly reversed the tide of the war through his landing at Inchon was now no longer the man at the helm as the war entered a new phase. The next battle lasted two years and was one of the most challenging of the war, but unlike previous battles, this would take place around a negotiating table.

Chapter 8 – The Bloody Ceasefire and Looming Bomb

The next phase of the war began in June 1951. The Soviet Union representative to the UN submitted a proposal that ceasefire discussions between the parties involved in the Korean conflict should begin. Truman agreed and chose to send Vice Admiral Charles Turner Joy to represent UN interests. Lieutenant General Nam Il would represent the North Korean communists[clxvi] and the talks began on 10 July in the ancient Korean capital of Kaesong, in the south of the peninsula on the 38th parallel.

The Long Haggle

Peace talks did not begin smoothly. Syngman Rhee refused to agree to any armistice and the peninsula remained divided[clxvii]. Initial talks underwent frequent suspensions. Neither side could agree on the locations of the demarcation lines, the course of action to take for prisoners of war, or even the location of the peace talks, and the talks relocated to Panmunjom on the north of the peninsula shortly after they began.

The issue was there was no longer a real thirst to bring the conflict to a speedy resolution. With battlefield lines stable, neither side was suffering large scale loss of life. The war could have ended in 1951 once the positions around the 38th parallel were assumed, but it would drag on for another two years before any semblance of peace was reached.

Part of the problem was the Soviet Union had no desire for peace in Korea. The Cold War in Europe was heating up and Stalin wanted to keep American attention on Asia.[clxviii] However, it wasn't just the Soviet pressure on China to keep the war going that caused the negotiations to drag on. Truman was preparing for a general election in 1952, and didn't want to appear to be soft on communism. Truman had to push for the most favorable conditions for the Americans or he would have been crucified in the elections[clxix]. As a result, the armistice would have to wait until Eisenhower took the presidency, who would have a stronger mandate and could afford to be a little more conciliatory in the negotiations. These reasons, along with Syngman Rhee's contempt for the negotiations and his attempts to undermine them by arbitrarily releasing prisoners of war to change the conditions of the situation[clxx], it is little surprise they took as long as they did and incredible that a meaningful ceasefire could be agreed on at all.

The Prisoner of War Issue

When negotiations began, one of the sticking points was the question of what to do with the POWs held by both sides. Many of the Chinese and North Korean prisoners held in South Korea had expressed a reluctance to return home. The U.S. estimated that as many as 116,000 out of the 132,000 Chinese and North Korean POWs did not want to return to their home countries[clxxi].

This estimate proved to be wildly inflated. But this did not stop President Truman from insisting on the condition that POWs be allowed to choose whether they would return home or settle in their host nation[clxxii]. He believed this was an opportunity to undermine the communist governments of North Korea and China on the world stage. However, several senior members of his administration were vehemently against this condition, including Charles Turner Joy. They feared the communists would use this as an excuse to hold onto American prisoners or use it to infiltrate the ROK and the U.S. with communist sympathizers.

Mao was also against this condition. He feared Chiang Kai-shek was using this as a strategy to indoctrinate Chinese troops and expand his nationalist power base. After the U.S. conducted a survey among prisoners of war, it appeared Mao was right to be concerned. Sixteen thousand out of 21,000 Chinese prisoners in South Korea said they didn't want to return home to the People's Republic of China, far more than among KPA prisoners[clxxiii].

With Truman insisting on the inclusion of the condition and Mao so ferociously against it, the topic of prisoners of war became a severe source of delay in the ceasefire negotiations.

Both sides were so suspicious of the other on the issue of prisoners of war that even after a settlement was reached in June 1953 and ROKA prisoners were returned, Syngman Rhee's government put them through six more months of political re-education before they could return home to their families across South Korea[clxxiv]. He feared they had been indoctrinated by the communists and sent back to cause unrest in South Korea.

Truman, Eisenhower and the threat of nuclear annihilation

John Foster Dulles, the U.S. Secretary of State under Eisenhower, remained adamant it was the Eisenhower administration's decision to threaten the expansion of the war to include nuclear weapons that brought peace to the peninsula[clxxv]. However, there is significant evidence to suggest that this hindered negotiations rather than hastened them.

Nuclear weapons had first been considered as early as November 1950[clxxvi], when Truman issued a public statement suggesting that the nuclear option was on the table. Not only did this fail to prevent the Chinese from entering the war, but it also failed to prevent them chasing the retreating U.S. forces into the south of the peninsula and taking Seoul.

Each time the threats of nuclear destruction occurred, the Chinese responded more defiantly against American conditions in the negotiations. In 1952, while Truman was frantically trying to negotiate favorable ceasefire conditions to give him momentum going into the elections, he issued an ultimatum to the Chinese. They either agreed to the latest package detailing the conditions for POW release or they could expect a rainfall of bombs and ruin from the air. At the time, the Indian Prime Minister Nehru was in the process of constructing a POW package that looked hopeful to both the Chinese and Americans, but once the ultimatum was given, the Chinese rejected the package outright[clxxvii].

When Truman lost the 1952 Presidential Election and Eisenhower was making preparations to enter the White House in January 1953, he visited Korea. It was during this trip he formulated his diplomatic approach. When he returned from Korea in December 1952, Eisenhower decided his Korea strategy would encompass two core key courses of action. The first was he would not tolerate any more delays to the peace talks. The second was the only military plans he would endorse to end the diplomatic deadlock would be through the deployment of nuclear weapons[clxxviii].

Once inaugurated in January 1953, Eisenhower increased atomic testing in a gesture to show China the extent of U.S. aerial capabilities[clxxix]. However, once again, this caused China to back away from an armistice. In response to Eisenhower's bullish approach, in February the CCP sent a leading nuclear scientist to Moscow and appealed to Stalin for immediate nuclear retaliation in the event of a nuclear strike on China from the U.S. The answer they received was never disclosed but the Soviet Union certainly never publicly ruled this out or contradicted Mao on the matter[clxxx]. This closed-door appeal to Stalin was supported by a public declaration by Zhou Enlai on 4 February that China would fight on should Eisenhower wish to escalate the war[clxxxi]. The Chinese media also indicates the widely held belief that Eisenhower's threats were nothing more than political bluster, as Truman's had been before.

The more noise Eisenhower made, the more China were determined they would hold the line at the 38th parallel and not be pushed over at the negotiating table. The U.S. was forced to make concessions when the nuclear threats were at their peak. In February, Eisenhower dropped a hundred tons of ordnance on North Korea, the most intense bombing the country had received in over a year[clxxxii]. There seemed to progress occurring after this as in March, Zhou Enlai made the concession that any Chinese prisoners of war who didn't want to return to China could be transferred to a neutral state. This was serious progress on the prisoner of war issue, which had plagued the negotiations since 1951. Then on 20 May the National Security Council publicly recommended the use of atomic weapons and the Chinese, once again, rejected the proposals and forced the U.S. to drop the clause to progress with the negotiations[clxxxiii].

The problem was Eisenhower's threats were transparent. He was still making nuclear threats almost two years after the decision had been made by Truman to open peace negotiations. With the wheels of peace in motion the Chinese knew the U.S. would have nothing to gain by escalating the war once more[clxxxiv]. Mao was also acutely aware the U.S. would never sit down to peace negotiations unless the Chinese had already asserted their dominance on the battlefield. There were also the objectives of the United States' closest ally, the British government, to think about. The British relied on trade with China to maintain their Hong Kong colony. The use of atomic weapons against China lead to strained relations with the British, who had helped the American campaign in Korea and had proven themselves to be useful allies[clxxxv].

As the negotiations drew on, Eisenhower attempted to bring Syngman Rhee on board to try and hasten the process. He offered the South Korean leader significant benefits in the form of a postwar defense agreement and promised to unlock more postwar aid to for the South Koreans, but Rhee still refused to be any part of an armistice agreement[clxxxvi]. In June 1953, as an armistice seemed inevitable, Rhee once again tried to sabotage the process by releasing 25,000 prisoners of war. In accordance with Eisenhower's zero tolerance policy on unnecessary delays, he drew up 'Operation Everready'[clxxxvii] which involved the removal of Rhee in a coup d'état, should he pull a similar stunt again. Fortunately for Rhee, the order to carry out the coup was never given.

After two final failed communist offensives in June, the three parties in negotiations came to an armistice agreement. On 27 June the Chinese, U.S., and North Korean parties agreed to the installation of a 2.5-mile buffer zone along the 38th parallel and the peninsula was carved up across the demarcation line that still holds to this day[clxxxviii]. More than two years of negotiations came to an end. However, there was no formal peace agreement drawn up and the South Korean government never agreed to the ceasefire, so technically the Korean War is still in progress today.

Chapter 9 – The Legacy of the Korean War

The Korean conflict claimed a total of around 4 million casualties, with at least half of these coming from civilians. In the 20th century, only the First and Second World Wars claimed more lives than the Korean conflict[clxxxix]. Despite this, and the 36,940 U.S. servicemen killed[cxc], the Korean War is still often forgotten in the American narrative of the twentieth century. Its timing, sandwiched between World War II and the Vietnam War, means it is often overlooked. However, the Korean War forged the landscape of the Korean peninsula today and set the tone for how the U.S. would deal with communist expansion across the globe.

Part of the reason why the conflict is so often overlooked in the West, is that warfare is usually remembered by the impact on the domestic situation at home[cxci]. The Vietnam

War is often remembered for its impact on the Civil Rights movement and the particularly heated public protests and debates. In comparison, the Korean War is often viewed as having a relatively limited impact on domestic policy in the U.S. But this couldn't be further from the truth.

Shaping U.S. Cold War Policy

The impact of the Korean conflict on U.S. foreign policy cannot be overstated. The conflict represented the birth of the American policy of militarized containment that would stay with them for most of the Cold War period[cxcii]. Truman's notion the deployment of the American military was essential for preventing the spread of communism was applied to the Vietnam in the '50s and '60ssixties, then again against Cuba at the Bay of Pigs invasion and dictated the tone for most of the Cold War.

Sino-American relations had been irreversibly changed in the wake of the Korean war. At the start of the Korean War, Truman used the conflict to shoehorn in a new American policy towards China. The 7th Fleet was dispatched to the Taiwan Straits to secure Taiwan and prevent Mao's takeover of the island[cxciii]. This would put Sino-American relations on ice for the next 20 years until they thawed under the Nixon administration in the '70s. The independence of Taiwan is still a source of contention across China today. Truman's decision to secure it has had a marked effect on the history of modern China.

The Korean War was the first real test of UN bipartisanship and resolve. The boycott from the Soviet Union on the UN Security Council Vote on intervention in Korea meant the U.S. could embark on a campaign against communism in Korea under the banner of the UN. However, in the wake of the decision to intervene, the U.S. was acutely aware of their good fortune and understood that had the Soviet Union used their veto, they would have been denied the UN's approval. As a result, in October 1950, the 'United for Peace' Resolution was passed[cxciv]. This allowed the General Assembly to call on the member states to form a union to halt aggression, even if the communist states in the Security Council exercised their right to veto intervention. This changed the way the UN functioned, and still holds to this day, shifting some of the power away from the Security Council and into the General Assembly.

Before the Korean War, American foreign policy objectives were not always in line with their military capabilities. This was most acutely expressed by MacArthur's insistence on expanding the war, despite aerial and military capabilities preventing them from effectively doing so. Following the Chinese invasion and the destruction of MacArthur's two infantry columns, the war served to bring American foreign policy objectives further in line with American capabilities[cxcv].

This was achieved by a complete change in U.S. military policy and a dramatic increase in military funding during the Korean War and in the following years. NSC-68 was first presented to Truman in April 1950, before the outbreak of war. The recommendation called for Truman to vastly increase American spending on military procuration in response to the Soviet Union developing the atomic bomb in 1949. While Truman agreed to develop the hydrogen bomb in January 1950, he refused to endorse the expansive military investment NSC-68 was calling for[cxcvi].

After the war broke out and the American forces were in retreat, Truman gave his authorization to the recommendation. It quadrupled the U.S. defense budget, increasing it from $13 billion in June 1950 to $50 billion by the end of 1951, after China had crossed the Yalu and crushed US forces[cxcvii]. This affected the U.S. economy and forced Truman and Eisenhower to implement several of the economic policies which defined the U.S. economy of the twentieth century. The mandatory wage was introduced, as were price and credit controls, and contracts between private military firms and the U.S. government exploded[cxcviii]. The U.S. government became much more involved in the regulation of the U.S. economy, setting a precedent that would remain until Reagan's administration in the '80s when neo-liberalism prevailed.

The Korean War also influenced the U.S. on a level deeper than government policy. It altered the relationship between the President and Congress. During the Korean War, Truman had been able to commit the United States Military to a full-scale war on foreign soil without a congressional mandate. This idea of an "imperial presidency[cxcix]" was introduced. Truman had set a precedent whereby the president could bypass Congress and commit the U.S. military to war under cover of a national security threat. Lyndon B. Johnson would go on to do the same thing in Vietnam to commit the United States to a war there just a few years later.

Forgotten Lessons

There were other lessons to be taken from Korea. The peace negotiations and the decision to cross the 38th parallel in the weeks after the Inchon landing demonstrated that going into a conflict without an exit plan or a clear objective for success was a recipe for disaster. Yet the U.S. would make the same mistakes again in Vietnam, the Philippines, Germany and then again most recently in Afghanistan and Iraq. Getting into a war is easy: getting out of it is the hard part. The U.S. would continue to enter conflicts it couldn't get out of throughout the twentieth and into the twenty-first centuries. Incredibly, more than 30,000 troops[cc] are still garrisoned in South Korea today, a full sixty-four years after the end of the Korean War.

The North Korean guerilla-style warfare caused the allied forces real problems in the summer of 1950 and the much smaller Communist forces pushed the U.S. back to the Pusan perimeter thanks to their discipline and difficult guerilla strategies. The Vietnamese would adopt similar strategies in the Vietnam War a few years later, with the same level of success, indicating the U.S. military had still not developed a coherent military strategy to deal with guerilla-style warfare[cci]. The whole management of the Vietnam War would demonstrate the U.S. military had a short memory. From William Westmoreland's parallels to Douglas MacArthur, to Nixon's echoes of Eisenhower's nuclear threats. Had the U.S. military learned from their conduct in Korea, they would have avoided many of the pitfalls they would later fall into in Vietnam.

A Korean War for A Korean Future

Although the War was of paramount importance on U.S. policy throughout the twentieth century, it should be remembered the Korean War was a civil war between the Korean population, fought by Koreans, for the future of the peninsula.

The loss of life across Korea was catastrophic. South Korea reported 415,004 deaths with 1,312,836 injured by the end of the conflict. On the communist side, North Korean casualties reached two million, with one million injured civilians, 520,000 dead North Korean soldiers and 900,000 Chinese fatalities[ccii].

Kim and Rhee finished the conflict more powerful than before. Kim had proven himself in war and most of his political rivals had died during the conflict, while Rhee had protected the South from a Chinese invasion[cciii]. If anything, divides between the two Koreas had been deepened both politically and geographically as the buffer zone sealed the fate of the Korean landscape and prevented any contact occurring between the two sides.

This demarcation line along the 38th parallel and the implications for the future of Korea is the single largest legacy of the Korean War. Not only did it carve up the geography of the peninsula, but it carved up a national population and their families. Ten million people[cciv] still live in the South and do not know if their family members living in the North are still alive. They have not had contact with them since the end of the war.

The Korean War was not just a proxy war for the U.S. and the Soviet Union, as it is often referred to in the West. It was a national people's struggle for a revolution. An understanding of the Korean conflict is essential for understanding the Korean peninsula today. The North Korean state media continue to spew vitriolic bile daily about South Korean politicians and their relationship with the U.S.[ccv]. The South Korean government continue to host joint military exercises with the U.S. military annually. The Korean War is the lens through which all relationships on the peninsula today must be viewed.

Talks did occur between the two Koreas in the 1970s, 1984, and then again in 1990, but each time there was no agreement reached for notions of reconciliation. Both sides still regard the other with suspicion and old wounds are yet to heal. However, these wounds will not heal on their own and, moving forward, open communication is essential to prevent another flare up of hostilities and to bring the arrival of any semblance of cooperation on the peninsula.

Korea still has a long way to go to repair the anguish felt on the peninsula. The Korean War is a story of separation, from familial separation, political separation, national separation, to geographical separation. Both North and South Korean leaders had the objective of achieving a unified Korean peninsula, but sixty-four years later and the last legacy of the war couldn't be further from unification.

Conclusion

In Korean tradition, *Changsung* guardian poles were erected at the entrance to villages and pathways to protect the villagers against evil spirits. They still litter the rural Korean landscape today. The intricately carved, intimidating visages etched into the wood appeal to spiritual forces for protection and security. They are adorned to symbolize both male and female spirits, representing an equilibrium between gender and good vs evil.

The dichotomy of *Changsung* is something essentially Korean. The Korean War is no exception. The peninsula fell under two vastly different competing political ideologies, backed by two global superpowers. Even the North Korean government in exile had two components: the Provisional government in China and Kim's Soviet exiles. The equilibrium Kim balanced between Mao and Stalin brought the war to fruition. These dichotomies dictated the tide and order of the conflict and maintained an almost mystical hold over the peninsula.

The legacy of the Korean War has been most profoundly felt in relationships: the relationships between the North and South; the relationship between the North and China, which continues to play out in the media as Beijing continues to circumvent UN imposed sanctions on North Korea; at a familial level, the relationships between family members between living in the north of the peninsula and those living in the south were irrevocably destroyed and contact was severed for generations to come.

Not only was the war one of the most physically destructive of the twentieth century, but it also irreversibly altered Korean national identity. Had the United States never gotten involved, Korea may have been able to preserve these relationships and their pre-1945 national identity. They would have had their Civil War and one political ideology might have engulfed the other and the situation could have been resolved. What makes Korea one of the saddest wars of the twentieth-century is that it solved nothing. The 38th parallel still stands today and the immense loss of life didn't alter the geographical or political stance of the peninsula.

Despite the tragedy and destruction that came from the war and the relationships it destroyed, there are some stories of immense love and reconciliation that came from the Korean War. The town of Kurim is one such story.

Kurim was a small town in the southwest of the country. During the Korean War, the population took up pitchforks and hoes and attacked each other, with some of the town's population sympathizing with the communists and others supporting the Rhee government. More than 300 people died in the skirmishes[ccvi], leaving almost every household in the town affected and grieving. Following the war, conditions were ripe for revenge and a breeding ground of hostility. However, the town refused to let an air of vengeance and turmoil prevail. In 2006, the village published a comprehensive history of Kumin. Although they listed those who died in the conflicts, they refused to print any information alluding to whom had killed who in the conflict. The village elders decided the best way to move forward for the town was to keep the details of who was responsible for which murders a secret.

These small acts of reconciliation may one day snowball into reconciliation on a macro-level. But for the time being, the relationships on the Korean peninsula remain racked by the ghosts of the war, and they show no sign of abetting.

Can you help me?

If you enjoyed this book, then I'd really appreciate it if you would post a short review on Amazon. I read all the reviews myself so that I can continue to provide books that people want.

Thanks for your support!

Preview of World War 2

A Captivating Guide from Beginning to End

Introduction

The Second World War was one of the most traumatic events in human history. Across the world, existing conflicts became connected, entangling nations in a vast web of violence. It was fought on land, sea, and air, touching every inhabited continent. Over 55 million people died, some of them combatants, some civilians caught up in the violence, and some murdered by their own governments.

It was the war that unleashed the Holocaust and the atomic bomb upon the world. But it was also a war that featured acts of courage and self-sacrifice on every side.

The world would never be the same again.

Chapter 1 – The Rising Tide

The Second World War grew out of conflicts in two parts of the world: Europe and East Asia. Though the two would eventually become entangled, it's easier to understand the causes of the war by looking at them separately.

Europe's problems were rooted in centuries of competition between powerful nations crammed together on a small and densely populated continent. Most of the world's toughest, most stubborn, and most ambitious kids were crammed together in a single small playground. Conflict was all but inevitable.

The most recent large European conflict had been the First World War. This was the first industrialized war, a hugely traumatic event for all the participants. In the aftermath, Germany was severely punished for its aggression by the victorious Allied powers. The remains of the Austro-Hungarian empire fell apart, creating instability in the east. And the Russian Empire, whose government had been overthrown during the turmoil of the war, became the Union of Soviet Socialist Republics (USSR), the first global power to adopt the new ideology of communism.

From this situation of instability, a new form of politics emerged. Across Europe, extreme right-wing parties adopted ultra-nationalistic views. Many of them incorporated ideas of racial superiority. Most were strongly influenced by the fear of communism. All relied on scapegoating outsiders to make themselves more powerful.

The first to reach prominence was the Fascist Party in Italy under Benito Mussolini. Mussolini was a veteran soldier, gifted orator, and skilled administrator. He rallied disenchanted left-wingers and those who felt put down by corrupt politicians and forceful trade unions. Using a mixture of persuasion and intimidation, he won the 1922 election and became prime minister. Through a series of laws, he turned his country into a one-party dictatorship. Most of his achievements were domestic, bringing order and efficiency at the price of freedom, but he also had ambitions abroad. He wanted Italy to be a colonial power like Britain or France, and so in 1935-6 his forces conquered Abyssinia.

Mussolini was surpassed in almost every way by the man who reached power in Germany a decade later—Adolph Hitler. A decorated veteran of the First World War, Hitler was embittered at the Versailles Treaty, which imposed crushing restrictions upon Germany in the aftermath of the war. He developed a monstrous ideology that combined racism, homophobia, and a bitter hatred of communism. Like Mussolini, he brought together oratory and street violence to seize control of Germany. Once elected chancellor in 1933, he purged all opposition and had himself made Führer, the nation's "leader" or "guide." He then escalated the rearmament of Germany, casting off the shackles of Versailles.

Hitler and Mussolini intervened in the Spanish Civil War of 1936-9. Rather than have their nations join the war, they sent parts of their armed forces to support Franco's right-wing armies, testing new military technology and tactics while ensuring the victory of a man they expected to be an ally—a man who would in fact keep his nation out of the coming war for Europe.

Meanwhile, Hitler was playing a game of chicken with the other European powers. In March 1936, he occupied the Rhineland, a part of Germany that had been demilitarized after the war. Two years later, he annexed his own homeland of Austria, with its large German-speaking population. He occupied parts of Czechoslovakia that fall and finished the job off the following spring. At every turn, the rest of Europe backed down rather than go to war to protect less powerful nations.

Meanwhile, in Asia, the Chinese revolutions of 1911 and 1913, along with the Chinese Civil

War that broke out in 1927, had triggered a parallel period of instability. Nationalists and communists battled for control of a vast nation, destroying the regional balance of power.

Japan was a nation on the rise. Economic growth had created a sense of ambition which had then been threatened by a downturn in the 1930s. Interventions by Western powers, including their colonies in Asia and a restrictive naval treaty of 1930, embittered many in Japan, who saw the Europeans and Americans as colonialist outsiders meddling in their part of the world.

The Japanese began a period of expansion, looking to increase their political dominance and their control of valuable raw resources. They invaded Chinese Manchuria in 1931 and from then on kept encroaching on Chinese territory. At last, in 1937, the Chinese nationalist leader Chiang Kai-Shek gave up on his previous policy of giving ground to buy himself time. A minor skirmish escalated into the Second Sino-Japanese War.

From an Asian point of view, the war had already begun. But it would be Hitler who pushed Europe over the brink and gave the war its Western start date of 1939.

Check out this book!

Make sure to check out more books by Captivating History

Free Bonus from Captivating History (Available for a Limited time)

Hi History Lovers!

Now you have a chance to join our exclusive history list so you can get your first history ebook for free as well as discounts and a potential to get more history books for free! Simply visit the link below to join.

Captivatinghistory.com/ebook

Also, make sure to follow us on:

Twitter: @Captivhistory

Facebook: Captivating History: @captivatinghistory

Sources

[i] Kawasaki, Yutaka. "Was the 1910 Annexation Treaty Between Korea and Japan Concluded Illegally", *Murdoch University Electronic Journal of Law*, 3,2 (1996).
http://www.murdoch.edu.au/elaw/issues/v3n2/kawasaki.html. [Accessed 1 Aug 2017]

[ii] McNamara, Dennis L. *The Colonial Origins of Korean Enterprise: 1910-1945* (Cambridge: Cambridge University Press: 1990) p.36

[iii] Savada, Andrea Matles and Shaw, William. Eds. *South Korea: A Country Study* (Washington: GPO for the Library of Congress: 1990)
http://countrystudies.us/south-korea/7.htm
Accessed: [1 Aug 2017]

[iv] McNamara, Dennis L. *The Colonial Origins of Korean Enterprise: 1910-1945* (Cambridge: Cambridge University Press: 1990) p.36

[v] Savada, Andrea Matles and Shaw, William. Eds. *South Korea: A Country Study* (Washington: GPO for the Library of Congress: 1990) http://countrystudies.us/south-korea/7.htm Accessed: [1 Aug 2017]

[vi] McNamara, Dennis L. *The Colonial Origins of Korean Enterprise: 1910-1945* (Cambridge: Cambridge University Press: 1990) p.34

[vii] McNamara, Dennis L. *The Colonial Origins of Korean Enterprise: 1910-1945* (Cambridge: Cambridge University Press: 1990) p.36

[viii] Savada, Andrea Matles and Shaw, William. Eds. *South Korea: A Country Study* (Washington: GPO for the Library of Congress: 1990) http://countrystudies.us/south-korea/7.htm Accessed: [1 Aug 2017]

[ix] McNamara, Dennis L. *The Colonial Origins of Korean Enterprise: 1910-1945* (Cambridge: Cambridge University Press: 1990) p.36

[x] Savada, Andrea Matles and Shaw, William. Eds. *South Korea: A Country Study* (Washington: GPO for the Library of Congress: 1990) http://countrystudies.us/south-korea/7.htm [Accessed: 1 Aug 2017]

[xi] McNamara, Dennis L. *The Colonial Origins of Korean Enterprise: 1910-1945* (Cambridge: Cambridge University Press: 1990) p.36

[xii] Savada, Andrea Matles and Shaw, William. Eds. *South Korea: A Country Study* (Washington: GPO for the Library of Congress: 1990) http://countrystudies.us/south-korea/7.htm [Accessed: 1 Aug 2017]

[xiii] Pang, Kie-chung, *Landlords, Peasants and Intellectuals in Modern Korea* (Ithaka, NY: Cornell University: 2005)

[xiv] Millet, Alan R. "The Korean People Missing in Action in the Misunderstood War, 1845-1954" in Stueck, Wiliam, ed. *The Korean War in World History* (Kentucky: University Press of Kentucky: 2004) p.13

[xv] Ibid. P.17

[xvi] Ibid.

[xvii] Ibid. P.18

[xviii] Ibid

[xix] Liu, Xiaoyuan, "Sino-American Diplomacy over Korea During World War II" in *The Journal of American-East Asian Relations*, 1, 2 (1992) p.233

[xx] Ibid

[xxi] Millet, Alan R. "The Korean People Missing in Action in the Misunderstood War, 1845-1954" in

Stueck, Wiliam, ed. *The Korean War in World History* (Kentucky: University Press of Kentucky: 2004) p.17

[xxii] Daws, Gavan, *Prisoners of the Japanese: POWs of World War II in the Pacific* (New York: W. Morrow: 1994)

[xxiii] Shoten, Iwanami, *Comfort Women: Sexual Slavery in Japanese Military During World War II*, (New York: Columbia University Press: 2000)

[xxiv] Williamson, Lucy, 'Comfort Women: South Korea's Survivors of Japanese Brothels', *BBC News*, 2013, http://www.bbc.com/news/magazine-22680705, [Accessed 3 Aug, 2017]

[xxv] Ibid.

[xxvi] Liu, Xiaoyuan, 'Sino-American Diplomacy over Korea during World War II', *The Journal of American-East Asian Relations*, 1, 2, 1992, p.227

[xxvii] Ibid. p.226

[xxviii] Ibid. p.233

[xxix] Ibid. p.243

[xxx] Ibid. p.244

[xxxi] Ibid. p.247

[xxxii] Ibid. p.254

[xxxiii] Ibid. p.259

[xxxiv] Ibid.

[xxxv] Barry, Mark P. 'The US and the 1945 Division of Korea: Mismanaging the "Big Decisions"', *International Journal on World Peace*, 29,4, 2012, p.42

[xxxvi] Ibid. P.43

[xxxvii] Lee, Won Sul, *The United States and the Division of Korea*, (Seoul: Kyunghee University Press: 1982) pp.68-69

[xxxviii] Barry, Mark P. 'The US and the 1945 Division of Korea: Mismanaging the "Big Decisions"', *International Journal on World Peace*, 29,4, 2012, p.44

[xxxix] Ibid. pp.46-47

[xl] Ibid. p.49

[xli] Ibid.

[xlii] Editorial, 'Ghosts of Cheju', *Newsweek*, 2000, http://www.newsweek.com/ghosts-cheju-160665 [Accessed 6 Aug 2017]

[xliii] Cummings, Bruce, *The Korean War: a History*, (New York: Random House: 2010), p.106

[xliv] Savada, Andrea Matles and Shaw, William. Eds. *South Korea: A Country Study* (Washington: GPO for the Library of Congress: 1990) http://countrystudies.us/south-korea/7.htm [Accessed: 1 Aug 2017]

[xlv] Lee, Chong-Sik, 'Politics in North Korea: Pre-Korean War Stage', *the China Quarterly*, 14, 1963, pp 3-16

[xlvi] Savada, Andrea Matles and Shaw, William. Eds. *South Korea: A Country Study* (Washington: GPO for the Library of Congress: 1990) http://countrystudies.us/south-korea/7.htm [Accessed: 1 Aug 2017]

[xlvii] Central Intelligence Agency, *North and South Korea: Separate Paths of Economic Development*, ER IM 72-82, 1972. < https://www.cia.gov/library/readingroom/docs/CIA-RDP85T00875R001700030082-7.pdf> [Accessed on 13 Aug 2017]

[xlviii] Savada, Andrea Matles and Shaw, William. Eds. *South Korea: A Country Study* (Washington: GPO for the Library of Congress: 1990) http://countrystudies.us/south-korea/7.htm [Accessed: 1 Aug 2017]

[xlix] Ibid.

[l] Ibid.

[li] Ibid.

[lii] Merril, John Roscoe, 'The Cheju-do Rebellion', *Journal of Korean Studies*, 2, 1, 1980, pp.139-197

[liii] Editorial, 'Ghosts of Cheju', *Newsweek*, 2000, http://www.newsweek.com/ghosts-cheju-160665 [Accessed 6 Aug 2017]

[liv] Ibid.

[lv] Savada, Andrea Matles and Shaw, William. Eds. *South Korea: A Country Study* (Washington: GPO for the Library of Congress: 1990) http://countrystudies.us/south-korea/7.htm [Accessed: 1 Aug 2017]

[lvi] Lee, Chong-Sik, 'Politics in North Korea: Pre-Korean War Stage', *the China Quarterly*, 14, 1963, p.3

[lvii] Ibid. p.4

[lviii] Ibid.

[lix] Ibid. p.9

[lx] Ibid. p.4

[lxi] Ibid. p.5

[lxii] Ibid. p. 5

[lxiii] Lankov, Andrei, *The Real North Korea: Life and Politics in the Failed Stalinist Utopia*, (Oxford: Oxford University Press, 2014) p.9

[lxiv] Lee, Chong-Sik, 'Politics in North Korea: Pre-Korean War Stage', *the China Quarterly*, 14, 1963, p.5

[lxv] Ibid. p13

[lxvi] Savada, Andrea Matles, ed., *North Korea: A Country Study*, (Washington: GPO for the Library

of Congress, 1993)
<http://countrystudies.us/north-korea/>
[Accessed 13 Aug 2017]

[lxvii] Ibid.

[lxviii] Lee, Chong-Sik, 'Politics in North Korea: Pre-Korean War Stage', *the China Quarterly*, 14, 1963, p.8

[lxix] Savada, Andrea Matles, ed., *North Korea: A Country Study*, (Washington: GPO for the Library of Congress, 1993)
<http://countrystudies.us/north-korea/>
[Accessed 13 Aug 2017]

[lxx] Ibid. p.9

[lxxi] Ibid.

[lxxii] Ibid. p.13

[lxxiii] Shtykov, Terenti, 'Telegram from Shtykov to Vyshinsky,' September 3, 1949, *Digital Archive: International History Declassified*, Wilson Center, <http://digitalarchive.wilsoncenter.org/document/112129> [Accessed 15 Aug 2017]

[lxxiv] Communist Party of the Soviet Union Politburo, 'September 24, 1949 Politburo Decision to Confirm the Following Directive to the Soviet Ambassador in Korea,' *Digital Archive: International History Declassified*, Wilson Center, <http://digitalarchive.wilsoncenter.org/document/112133>, [Accessed 15 Aug 2017]

[lxxv] Shtykov, Terenti, "Meeting between Stalin and Kim Il Sung," March 5, 1949, *Digital Archive: International History Declassified*, Wilson Center, <http://digitalarchive.wilsoncenter.org/document/112127> , [Accessed 15 Aug 2017]

[lxxvi] Millett, Allan R., *The War for Korea,1945-1950: A House Burning*, (Lawrence: University Press of Kansas, 2005), p.193

[lxxvii] Terenti Shtykov, "Meeting between Stalin and Kim Il Sung," March 5, 1949, *Digital Archive: International History Declassified*, Wilson Center, <http://digitalarchive.wilsoncenter.org/document/112127> , [Accessed 15 Aug 2017]

[lxxviii] Millett, Allan R. , *The War for Korea,1945-1950: A House Burning*, (Lawrence: University Press of Kansas, 2005), p.194

[lxxix] Kovalev, Ivan, 'Soviet Report on the Results of Chinese-Korean Talks on Military Cooperation,' May 18, 1949, *Digital Archive: International History Declassified*, Wilson Center <http://digitalarchive.wilsoncenter.org/document/114898> , [Accessed 15 Aug 2017]

[lxxx] Thornton, Richard C., *Odd Man Out: Truman, Stalin, Mao and the Origins of the Korean War*, (Washington, DC: Brassey's, 2001), p.2

[lxxxi] Shtykov, Terenti, 'Telegram Shtykov to Vyshinsky on a Luncheon at the Ministry of Foreign Affairs of the DPRK,' January 19, 1950, *Digital Archive: International History Declassified*, Wilson

Center, <http://digitalarchive.wilsoncenter.org/document/112135> , [Accessed 15 Aug 2017]

[lxxxii] Joseph Stalin, 'Telegram from Stalin to Shtykov,' January 30, 1950, *Digital Archive: International History Declassified*, Wilson Center, <http://digitalarchive.wilsoncenter.org/document/112136> , [Accessed 15 Aug 2017]

[lxxxiii] Thornton, Richard C., *Odd Man Out: Truman, Stalin, Mao and the Origins of the Korean War*, (Washington, DC: Brassey's, 2001), p.101

[lxxxiv] Ibid. p.102

[lxxxv] Ibid. p.103

[lxxxvi] Stueck, William, *Rethinking the Korean War: A New Diplomatic and Strategic History* (Princeton, NJ: Princeton University Press, 2002), p.73

[lxxxvii] Thornton, Richard C., *Odd Man Out: Truman, Stalin, Mao and the Origins of the Korean War*, (Washington, DC: Brassey's, 2001), p.2

[lxxxviii] Vyshinsky, Andrey, "Cable from Vyshinsky to Mao Zedong, Relaying Stalin's Stance on Permission for North Korea to attack South Korea."

[lxxxix] Stueck, William, *Rethinking the Korean War: A New Diplomatic and Strategic History* (Princeton, NJ: Princeton University Press, 2002), p.75

[xc] Gunther, John, *The Riddle of MacArthur*, (New York: Harper and Row: 1951), p.172

[xci] Gupta, Karunakar, 'How Did the Korean War Begin?', *China Quarterly*, 52, 1972, pp. 699-716, p.702

[xcii] Ibid.

[xciii] Stone, J.F., *The Hidden History of the Korean War*, (London: Turnstile Press: 1952), pp.46-7

[xciv] Gupta, Karunakar, 'How Did the Korean War Begin?', *China Quarterly*, 52, 1972, pp. 699-716, p.703

[xcv] Ibid. p.704

[xcvi] Ibid.

[xcvii] Ibid. 705

[xcviii] Ibid. pp.705-7

[xcix] Ibid. p.709

[c] Ibis. p.714

[ci] Allen, Richard C. , *Korea's Syngman Rhee* (Tokyo: Charles E. Cuttle Co., 1960), p. 117

[cii] Pritt, D. N., *New Light on Korea*, (London: Trinity Trust: 1951) pp.12-13

[ciii] Gupta, Karunakar, 'How Did the Korean War Begin?', *China Quarterly*, 52, 1972, pp. 699-716, p.703

[civ] Acheson to Johnson, 28 June 1950, FRUS, 1950, vol. 7: 217; Lindsay Memoran dum, 28 June 1950,

RG 218, CCS 383.21 Korea (3-19-45), Section 21, NA; *Truman, Years of Trial and Hope*, pp 340-41.

[cv] 'Drumright to Acheson, 29 June 1950, FRUS, 1950, vol. 7: 220; Schnabel, *Policy and Direction*, p.74.

[cvi] Appleman, Roy E., *South to the Naktong, North to the Yalu (June-November 1950),* (Washington, D.C.: Government Printing Office: 1961), pp.44-5

[cvii] Matray, James, 'America's Reluctant Crusade: Truman's Commitment of Combat Troops in the Korean War', *The Historian*, 42, 3, 1980, p.450

[cviii] Ibid. p.451

[cix] Ibid.

[cx] Park, Hong-Kyu, 'American Involvement in the Korean War', *The History Teacher,* 16, 2, 1983, pp.249-243, p.253

[cxi] Trussel, C.P., "Red Underground' in Federal Posts Alleged By Editor: In New Deal Era-Ex-Communist Names Algar Hiss, Then in State Department-Wallace Aides on List-Chambers Also Includes Former Treasury Official, White-Tells of Fears for His Life', *New York Times*, Aug 3, 1948

[cxii] Cummins Bruce, *The Korean War: A History*, (New York: Random House: 2010), pp.14-15

[cxiii] Ibid. p.15

[cxiv] Ibid. p.18

[cxv] Ibid.

[cxvi] Ibid. p.16

[cxvii] Ibid. pp.16-17

[cxviii] Ibid. p.18

[cxix] Ibid.

[cxx] Ibid.

[cxxi] Ibid. p.21

[cxxii] Stockwin, Harvey, 'MacArthur's Audacious Landing at Inchon Astounded Everyone- Except Mao', *The Japan Times*, 2000, <https://www.japantimes.co.jp/opinion/2000/09/21/commentary/world-commentary/macarthurs-audacious-landing-at-inchon-astounded-everyone-except-mao/#.WaB7kiiGPIV> , [Accessed 24 Aug 2017]

[cxxiii] Ibid.

[cxxiv] Ibid.

[cxxv] Ibid.

[cxxvi] Stockwin, Harvey, 'MacArthur's Audacious Landing at Inchon Astounded Everyone- Except Mao', *The Japan Times*, 2000, <https://www.japantimes.co.jp/opinion/2000/09/21/commentary/world-commentary/macarthurs-audacious-landing-at-inchon-astounded-everyone-

except-mao/#.WaB7kiiGPIV> , [Accessed 24 Aug 2017]

[cxxvii] Cummins Bruce, *The Korean War: A History*, (New York: Random House: 2010), p.19

[cxxviii] Ibid.

[cxxix] Stockwin, Harvey, 'MacArthur's Audacious Landing at Inchon Astounded Everyone- Except Mao', *The Japan Times*, 2000, <https://www.japantimes.co.jp/opinion/2000/09/21/commentary/world-commentary/macarthurs-audacious-landing-at-inchon-astounded-everyone-except-mao/#.WaB7kiiGPIV> , [Accessed 24 Aug 2017]

[cxxx] Cummins Bruce, *The Korean War: A History*, (New York: Random House: 2010), p.19

[cxxxi] National Security Council Report, NSC 81/1, "United States Courses of Action with Respect to Korea"," September 09, 1950, History and Public Policy Program Digital Archive, Truman Presidential Museum and Library <http://digitalarchive.wilsoncenter.org/document/116194>, [Accessed 24 Aug, 2017]

[cxxxii] Ibid.

[cxxxiii] Cummins Bruce, *The Korean War: A History*, (New York: Random House: 2010), p.22

[cxxxiv] Ibid. p.19

[cxxxv] Ibid. p.20

[cxxxvi] Ibid. p.23

[cxxxvii] Zhou, Bangning, 'Explaining China's Intervention in the Korean War in 1950', *Interstate- Journal of International Affairs*, 2015, 1

[cxxxviii] Cummins Bruce, *The Korean War: A History*, (New York: Random House: 2010), p.24

[cxxxix] Ibid.

[cxl] Ibid.

[cxli] Ibid.

[cxlii] Zhou, Bangning, 'Explaining China's Intervention in the Korean War in 1950', *Interstate- Journal of International Affairs*, 2015, 1

[cxliii] Cummins Bruce, *The Korean War: A History*, (New York: Random House: 2010), p.25

[cxliv] Ibid. pp.26-27

[cxlv] Ibid. p.28

[cxlvi] Ibid. p.25

[cxlvii] Garver, John W., 'Reviewed Works: China's Road to the Korean War: The Making of the Sino-American Confrontation' By Chen Jian, *The China Quarterly*, 1995, 144, p.1200

[cxlviii] Ibid.

[cxlix] Cummins Bruce, *The Korean War: A History*, (New York: Random House: 2010), p.28

[cl] Ibid. pp.27-28

[cli] Ibid. 29

[clii] Ibid.

[cliii] Brands, H.W., 'The Redacted Testimony that Fully Explains Why General MacArthur was Fired', *Smithsonian*, 2016, <http://www.smithsonianmag.com/history/redacted-testimony-fully-explains-why-general-macarthur-was-fired-180960622/> , [Accessed on 28 Aug 2017]

[cliv] Ibid.

[clv] Ibid.

[clvi] Ibid.

[clvii] Ibid.

[clviii] Ibid.

[clix] Ibid.

[clx] Hallion, Richard P., Cliff, Roger and Saunders, Phillip C., eds, *The Chinese Air Force: Evolving Concepts, Roles, and Capabilities*, (Washington D.C: National Defense University Press: 2012), p.73

[clxi] Brands, H.W., 'The Redacted Testimony that Fully Explains Why General MacArthur was Fired', *Smithsonian*, 2016, <http://www.smithsonianmag.com/history/redacte

d-testimony-fully-explains-why-general-macarthur-was-fired-180960622/> , [Accessed on 28 Aug 2017]

[clxii] Ibid.

[clxiii] Ibid.

[clxiv] Cummins Bruce, *The Korean War: A History*, (New York: Random House: 2010), p.156

[clxv] Ibid. p.157

[clxvi] Ibid. p.31

[clxvii] Ibid.

[clxviii] Ibid.

[clxix] Firedman, Edward, 'Nuclear Blackmail and the End of the Korean War'. *Modern China*, 1, 1, (1975), p.78

[clxx] Ibid. p.79

[clxxi] Foot, Rosemary J., 'Nuclear Coercion and the Ending of the Korean Conflict', *International Security*, 13, 3, (1989), p.96

[clxxii] Firedman, Edward, 'Nuclear Blackmail and the End of the Korean War'. *Modern China*, 1, 1, (1975), p.78

[clxxiii] Foot, Rosemary J., 'Nuclear Coercion and the Ending of the Korean Conflict', *International Security*, 13, 3, (1989), p.96

[clxxiv] Cummins Bruce, *The Korean War: A History*, (New York: Random House: 2010), p.33

[clxxv] Foot, Rosemary J., 'Nuclear Coercion and the Ending of the Korean Conflict', *International Security*, 13, 3, (1989), p.92

[clxxvi] Ibid. p.100

[clxxvii] Firedman, Edward, 'Nuclear Blackmail and the End of the Korean War'. *Modern China*, 1, 1, (1975), p.79

[clxxviii] Foot, Rosemary J., 'Nuclear Coercion and the Ending of the Korean Conflict', *International Security*, 13, 3, (1989), p.96

[clxxix] Cummins Bruce, *The Korean War: A History*, (New York: Random House: 2010), p.31

[clxxx] Firedman, Edward, 'Nuclear Blackmail and the End of the Korean War'. *Modern China*, 1, 1, (1975), p.82

[clxxxi] Ibid. p.83

[clxxxii] Foot, Rosemary J., 'Nuclear Coercion and the Ending of the Korean Conflict', *International Security*, 13, 3, (1989), p.97

[clxxxiii] Ibid.

[clxxxiv] Firedman, Edward, 'Nuclear Blackmail and the End of the Korean War'. *Modern China*, 1, 1, (1975), p.84

[clxxxv] Ibid. p.88

[clxxxvi] Cummins Bruce, *The Korean War: A History*, (New York: Random House: 2010), p.31

[clxxxvii] Ibid.

[clxxxviii] Ibid. p.34

[clxxxix] Millet, Alan R., 'Introduction to the Korean War', *The Journal of Military History*, 65, 4, (2001), p.923

[cxc] Cummins Bruce, *The Korean War: A History*, (New York: Random House: 2010), p.31

[cxci] Millet, Alan R., 'Introduction to the Korean War', *The Journal of Military History*, 65, 4, (2001), p.923

[cxcii] Pierpaoli Jr, Paul G., 'Beyond Collective Amnesia: A Korean War Retrospective', *International Social Science Review*, 76, 3-4, (2001), p.94

[cxciii] Ibid. p.95

[cxciv] Ibid. p.96

[cxcv] Ibid.

[cxcvi] Ibid.

[cxcvii] Ibid. p.97

[cxcviii] Ibid.

[cxcix] Ibid. p.99

[cc] Cummins Bruce, *The Korean War: A History*, (New York: Random House: 2010), p.231

[cci] Firedman, Edward, 'Nuclear Blackmail and the End of the Korean War'. *Modern China*, 1, 1, (1975), pp.76-77

[ccii] Cummins Bruce, *The Korean War: A History*, (New York: Random House: 2010), p.35

[cciii] Millet, Alan R., 'Introduction to the Korean War', *The Journal of Military History*, 65, 4, (2001), p.924

[cciv] Yoon, Young-Kwan, 'South Korea in 1999: Overcoming Cold War Legacies', *Asian Survey*, 40,1, (2000), p.164

[ccv] Millet, Alan R., 'Introduction to the Korean War', *The Journal of Military History*, 65, 4, (2001), p.932

[ccvi] Cummins Bruce, *The Korean War: A History*, (New York: Random House: 2010), p.236

ABOUT CAPTIVATING HISTORY

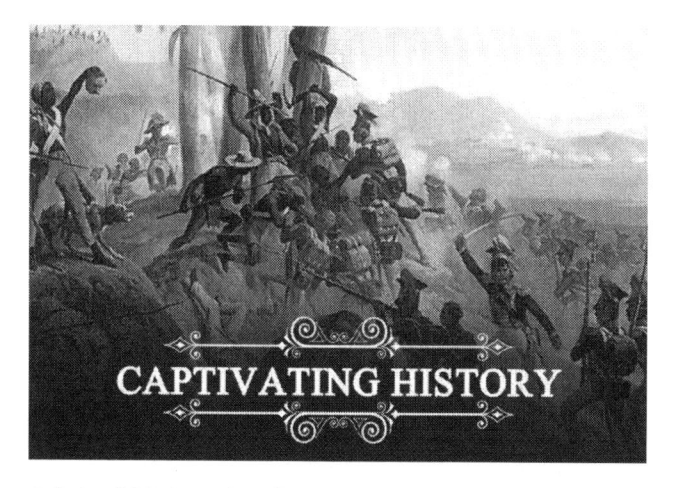

A lot of history books just contain dry facts that will eventually bore the reader. That's why Captivating History was created. Now you can enjoy history books that will mesmerize you. But be careful though, hours can fly by, and before you know it; you're up reading way past bedtime.

Get your first history book for free here:
http://www.captivatinghistory.com/ebook

Make sure to follow us on Twitter: @CaptivHistory and Facebook:
www.facebook.com/captivatinghistory so you can get all of our updates!

Printed in Great Britain
by Amazon